Understanding the Horse's Skin and Coat

Understanding the Horse's Skin and Coat

Jane Coatesworth

THE CROWOOD PRESS

First published in 2016 by
J.A. Allen

www.allenbooks.co.uk

JA Allen is an imprint of
The Crowood Press Ltd
Ramsbury, Marlborough
Wiltshire SN8 2HR

www.crowood.com

British Library Cataloguing-in-Publication Data
A catalogue record for this book is available from the British Library.

ISBN 978 1 908809 54 4

Photographs by the author, except where credited in the text
Frontispiece: Alice Loder (www.aliceloderphotography.co.uk)
Illustrations by Carole Vincer

Disclaimer
The contents of this book are for information only. They are not intended to replace professional diagnosis and treatment by a qualified veterinary surgeon. Please consult your vet about any concerns you may have about animals under your care.

Typeset by Jean Cussons Typesetting, Diss, Norfolk

Printed and bound in India by Replika Press Pvt. Ltd.

Contents

Acknowledgements

My grateful thanks and heartfelt appreciation for the love and counsel of my family and friends and for the kindness and support of many colleagues at the Animal Health Trust. I would also like to thank those people, credited in the text, who kindly gave me permission to use their photographs, and Richard Wilson for demonstrating his skills as a bow-maker. Finally, thanks to my patient companion throughout the typing process.

Author's Note

There are a couple of points to which I should draw the reader's attention.

Wherever, within the text, the heading Treatment Options appears, please be aware that what follows is strictly a list of *options*, each of which may be most appropriate to individual cases. Do not be tempted to use a treatment, or a combination of treatments at random. Please seek professional advice on the best treatment for your horse.

Those who read through the text in its entirety may notice that, in some cases, details of certain treatments may be repeated. This is because some treatments may be effective for more than one specific condition. Since readers may be seeking explanation of how best to treat an individual condition, it seemed helpful to include all details pertaining to that condition in one place, rather than direct the reader elsewhere in the text by means of cross-references.

Introduction

Imagine the shining coat, and flowing mane and tail, of a healthy, well-groomed horse as it catches the sunlight on a summer's day. These are beautiful things to see. The skin and coat are both attractive and interesting.

Many variable conditions affect the skin and the hair coat: internal variables such as hormones, blood supply and diet, and external variables such as infection, sunlight, parasites and rainfall. Add to this the numerous management options of rugs, clipping, grooming and housing. The skin is a dynamic organ that will respond to these variable factors, and to many more. Skin and hair are constantly replacing themselves, under the influence of genetic factors and of the changing internal and external environment.

A great advantage in dermatology is the ability to see, feel and smell what is happening at the surface of the skin. We can also see the part of the hair coat that is outside the hair follicles. A disadvantage in dermatology is that many skin conditions have a similar appearance. We are often working from a list of different conditions, all of which fit the history and appearance of the case. Our job is to work patiently through the list and to rule out, or to positively identify, each option. This patient and rigorous approach allows us to reach a definitive diagnosis. Having a diagnosis saves a lot of time and money in the long run: all subsequent treatment is rational and relevant. A diagnosis can also give a prognosis, allowing us to plan and budget realistically for ongoing care.

The management and treatment sections, which accompany the disease descriptions in this book, contain a number of options. These are not listed in order of preference. The best choice of options depends on the individual case, and is part of the clinical judgement required to manage a case successfully.

This book is not so much a diagnostic manual as an aid to understanding what we see in front of us when we look at a horse's skin and coat, both the normal and the diseased. Through that understanding we can make better decisions, which will lead to better actions and outcomes. Our individual and collective understanding changes as we see more of what is around us, and we integrate new information. The book is a source of information and discussion for the curious. It is for anyone who has wondered about the flies around a wound, or the lumps on that horse's skin, or why that foal turned out the colour he did.

1 People, Horses and Horsehair

HORSES AS AN HISTORICAL WORKFORCE

Horses were an essential workforce for many centuries. They were involved in military campaigns up to, and including, the Second World War. In addition to being cavalry mounts, horses hauled heavy guns, moved supplies and carried the wounded. It is estimated that eight million horses died in the First World War, plus countless mules and donkeys.

In civilian life, horses would have been a familiar part of daily life. They took over from oxen, to plough the fields, at the beginning of the nineteenth century. Horses hauled carts to bring in the harvest and to move timber. They pulled barges on the waterways. Ponies hauled coal in the pits. The doctor, the priest and the veterinary surgeon rode, or drove a trap, to and fro across the parish to make their visits. Towns and cities were packed with horses drawing cabs, trams and buses, with ponies pulling milk carts, and with heavy horses hauling the brewery drays. People rode or drove all manner of horses and horse-drawn vehicles for business and pleasure. Horses for riding and driving were available for hire by the day. Stage coaches and mail coaches were drawn by teams of two, four or six horses, depending on the terrain. The teams were changed at several stages during the day and the coach continued with fresh horses. Thousands of people were involved

Major C.D. Phillips, of the South Wales Borderers, mounted on the mare Longboat. Both survived the First World War. (Photo: A. Deacon)

USES OF HORSEHAIR

Plaster for walls
Suit linings
Rocking horse manes and tails
Cloth
Bows for stringed instruments
Sporrans
Ropes
Brushes
Leaders on Victorian era dry-fly fishing lines
Military plumes e.g. of the mounted regiment of the Household Cavalry of the British Army
Judicial wigs
Padding under shoulder armour
Filters for draining/clearing cider
Saddle stuffing

Brushes of various sizes, made of horsehair, and used for ink painting and other art work.

A short barrister's wig. (Photo: D. Hayes)

Mattress and window seat stuffing
Birds' nests in aviaries
Victorian hair lacework
Braiding on tunics
Scouring, with or without additional sand
Polishing wood and burnishing metal on a lathe
Padding First World War ammunition boxes
Attaching feathers to arrows
Gin traps for small birds
(Thanks to M. Sowden Sr for supplying this list)

in breeding and training horses to meet the demand for horse power, and in feeding and mucking out and handling horses. It is estimated that, in 1900, London had a working population of 300,000 horses.

The dependence on horse power, and the closely interdependent relationship between people and horses, came to a fairly swift end. In the UK horses were replaced for farm work, haulage and personal transport by the arrival of steam and coal power, and by the coming of the motor engine.

HORSEHAIR

Prior to their numerical decline, with so many horses around, and their relatively short working lifespan, there was a large volume of horsehair available. Horsehair was recognized as a tough and flexible material and was put to many creative uses. Some of these uses are discussed below.

Stuffing

Horsehair was widely used as a stuffing material. The durability and resilience of the material meant that it kept its shape well, while being somewhat flexible when loaded. Chairs, sofas, railway carriage seats, mattresses and saddles were all regularly stuffed with horsehair.

Horsehair stuffing protruding from beneath the covering layers at the back of an old sofa.

Horsehair Plaster

Before the adoption of plasterboard in the twentieth century, the interior walls of houses were frequently made with a lath and plaster technique. Lime-based plaster was mixed with chopped horse, or cattle, hair before being applied to the wooden laths. The addition of animal hair made the plaster stronger, and allowed it to stick more easily to the wooden laths. The hair was a lightweight and strengthening addition to the plaster.

Rocking Horse Manes and Tails

Rocking horses have been around as children's toys for many centuries. The earliest surviving English example is from around 1605, and can be seen in the Victoria & Albert Museum of Childhood. Rocking horses were popular in Victorian times. They were mass-produced for the home market and for export. F.H. Ayres was a leading London manufacturer of rocking horses, and other toys, around the turn of the twentieth century. The wooden horses had 'real' manes and tails, made either of horse or cattle hair. Modern rocking horses of traditional design, and restored period rocking horses, have manes and tails of flowing horsehair in a variety of natural and dyed colours.

The flowing horsehair mane and forelock of a traditional restored rocking horse. This example is a large, early, extra carved, original paint horse by F.H. Ayres. (Photo: rockinghorseheaven.com)

Suit Linings

Horsehair can be woven, with various amounts of cotton, into a fabric known in the tailoring profession as 'canvas'. Higher proportions of horsehair give a flatter, stiffer fabric, while more cotton allows greater flexibility and a rougher texture. The canvas provides the structure and shape of the garment, such as in a suit jacket. Horsehair canvas supports the overlying woollen fabric, allowing it to drape well, and maintains a flexible but consistent shape throughout the rigours of daily wear. The canvas middle layer is not seen in a finished garment, as it is covered with a silky lining material. Jackets can be half or fully canvassed, the former having horsehair material only across the chest and lapels. Horsehair canvas has largely been replaced by synthetic materials.

Horsehair Cloth

Cloth made from horsehair was widely produced during the nineteenth century. The warp was made of cotton and the weft of horse tail hair. The average length of a horse's tail limited the width of the cloth to approximately 70cm (28in). The fabric was flexible and hardwearing, and resistant to degradation by ultraviolet light. It was used for the upholstery of railway carriage seats and window blinds, and for household window seats and chairs.

Michael Sowden Sr finishing a hank of horse tail hair in the traditional manner. (Photo: M. Sowden Jr)

Horsehair cloth has an attractive sheen and can be dyed many colours. It was used by designers such as Charles Rennie Mackintosh for chair upholstery. Horsehair cloth is still woven today with a warp of cotton, or of polyester. There is a factory in Castle Cary, in Somerset, which has specialized in producing this product since 1837. The contemporary fabric is used both in restoration work, and in exclusive modern soft furnishing projects.

Bows for Stringed Instruments

The violin, viola, 'cello and double bass are all played by moving a bow across the strings to make the strings vibrate. The bow is a wooden, or carbon fibre, stick supporting between 100 and 150 horse tail hairs. The lower number of hairs would be appropriate, for example, in a period violin bow and would represent about 5g (0.18oz) of horsehair. The higher number of hairs would be found in a 'cello bow, of contemporary design, and would represent about 6g (0.2oz) of horsehair.

Bow-makers select the right number of hairs of an appropriate length, colour and quality. Each end of the selected hairs is then tied together with twine to form a bundle. One end of the bundle is trapped in the pointed end of the bow with a wooden wedge. Maple and lime-wood wedges are used to trap and spread out the hairs. The hair bundle is wetted, stretched and wedged

Hanks of white, black and mixed colour tail hair hanging in the workshop of the bow-maker.

The bow-maker has wedged the bundle of horse tail hair at the tip of the bow, and is now stretching and arranging it before securing it at the other end.

in at the other end of the bow. As the hairs dry they take up a uniform tension and form the flat 'ribbon' of parallel hairs used by the musician. The tension of the hair 'ribbon' can be adjusted by turning a screw in the end of the bow. With repeated use the hairs of a bow become worn and they lose their grip on the string. Bow-makers can then replace the worn hair bundle with a new one. Professional string players may have their bows re-haired two or three times each year.

2 What the Skin Does, and How it Does it

Structure and function are closely interrelated. The skin is the way it is, because of what it has needed to do over many generations of horses. In turn, it can perform the tasks it needs to, because of the way it is. The structure of the horse's skin is discussed first, to give a common descriptive language for when the function of the skin is discussed later. The separation of structure and function is helpful and convenient, but the two are interdependent.

STRUCTURE OF THE SKIN

The skin can be thought of as having two layers. These are the outer epidermal layer and the deeper dermal layer. Beneath these two layers is an underlying subcutaneous layer, literally a 'beneath the skin' layer.

The Epidermis

The epidermis is the outermost layer of the skin. The outer layer of the epidermis interacts directly with the wind and the weather. The epidermis contains skin cells called keratinocytes, which are made of the structural protein keratin. Keratin is a tough and fibrous material which comes in a number of forms. The keratin found in skin is softer than that in hoof or horn, or in a feather. The epidermis is a thin but essential layer. It has only, approximately, one-fiftieth the thickness of the underlying dermis.

Looking at a cross-section of the epidermis under the microscope we can conveniently divide it into a number of layers. The layers of the epidermis are described from the bottom layer towards the outside, as this is the direction in which the skin cells of the epidermis move and mature.

Basal Layer

The basal layer (*stratum basale*) of cells sits on the basement membrane. The basement membrane is a very thin structure, which divides the epidermis from the underlying dermis. It also anchors the epidermis firmly onto the dermis.

Keratinocytes

The keratinocytes of the basal layer have a plump, box-like shape. They are able to divide and to produce more keratinocytes. These

---

SKIN STRUCTURE – LAYERS OF TISSUE

From the body surface downwards:

Epidermis (A surface barrier layer)
Dermis (A connective tissue layer, containing smaller blood vessels)
Subcutaneous (A fibrous and fatty layer, containing larger blood vessels)
Beneath these layers are underlying muscle and bone

freshly made cells move outwards, away from the basement membrane. They change their shape, and their function, as they pass through the layers and towards the outside. Among the keratinocytes, in the basal layer, sit some other types of cell (melanocytes, Langerhans cells and Merkel cells). The epidermis does not have a blood supply. The cells of the basal layer are nourished by the adjacent underlying dermis. As keratinocytes move away from the basal layer, towards the skin surface, they die.

Melanocytes

Melanocytes are dendritic cells, literally having a tree-like or branching appearance. They have elongated arms, like an octopus or tree, which stretch out to communicate with neighbouring keratinocytes. Melanocytes make the different types of melanin which pigment the skin. The melanin is packaged up, and moved out to the ends of the elongated arms, where it is delivered to keratinocytes. Melanin may also be delivered to the root of a growing hair. The type and the amount of melanin in a keratinocyte, or in a hair, determines the colour of the horse's skin and hair coat.

Langerhans cells

These are part of the immune system. They are well placed, at the outer skin edge of the body, to encounter and interact with 'foreign' material. Examples of things that may be recognized as 'foreign' include ringworm infections, surface-living mites and bacteria. Langerhans cells pick up very small bits of this foreign material (antigen) and travel with them to a nearby lymph node. Here, the material is presented to other cells in the immune system, which then become activated and mount a response to the antigen.

Merkel cells

These are linked to nerves, and are associated with an awareness of touch on the skin. They may also have other functions, which are not yet fully understood. Horses have a high level of skin sensitivity and are very sensitive to touch.

Spinous Layer

The spinous layer (*stratum spinosum*) gets its name from the 'spines' that can be seen, at high magnification, reaching between the skin cells in this layer. These structures, which connect the cells, are called desmosomes. They anchor the cells firmly together, in three dimensions, and contribute to the cohesive and resilient nature of the skin. The spinous layer is three to five cells in thickness.

Granular Layer

The granular layer (*stratum granulosum*) is characterized by the presence of granules inside the keratinocytes. These granules contain bundles of structural proteins, which are being organized within the cell. The keratinocytes also produce proteins and lipids. As they move out of the granular layer they deposit the lipids outside the cell. This lipid material contributes to a flexible and water-repellent coating for the cells of the next layer (the horny layer). The granular layer is one to two cells in thickness.

Horny Layer

The horny layer (*stratum corneum*) is made up of thin, flattened cells embedded in a lipid-rich material. The horny layer can be envisaged as 'bricks and mortar'. The tough, flattened cells are the many layers of 'bricks' and the lipid-containing mixture is the surrounding 'mortar'. The whole is water-repellent, tough and flexible. The skin

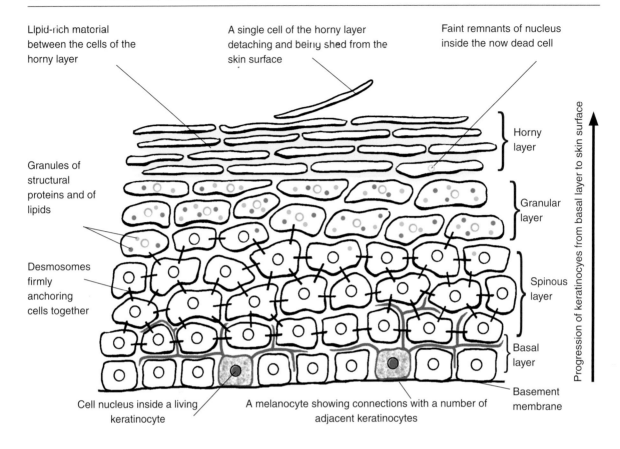

Lipid-rich material between the cells of the horny layer

A single cell of the horny layer detaching and being shed from the skin surface

Faint remnants of nucleus inside the now dead cell

Granules of structural proteins and of lipids

Desmosomes firmly anchoring cells together

Horny layer

Granular layer

Spinous layer

Basal layer

Basement membrane

Progression of keratinocyes from basal layer to skin surface

Cell nucleus inside a living keratinocyte

A melanocyte showing connections with a number of adjacent keratinocytes

The epidermis (not to scale). Merkel cells and Langerhans cells are not shown.

cells have, by this point, lost the tight bonds which attached them to their neighbours. They are shed into the environment at a rate which matches their production in the basal layer. This matched rate of production and shedding maintains the skin at an even level of thickness.

The Dermis

The dermis is a much thicker structure than the epidermis. It contains the hair follicles and their associated muscles, sweat glands and sebaceous glands. The dermis also contains sensory nerve endings and a complex web of interconnecting blood vessels. The robust structure of the dermis is provided by fibres of collagen and elastin, embedded in a gelatinous ground substance. Collagen, elastin and the ground substance are all produced by cells called **fibroblasts**. Fibroblasts have an elongated spindle shape and are very numerous in the dermis.

Skin has different degrees of thickness and elasticity at different sites of the body. This is largely because of variations in the density and arrangement of the collagen and the elastin fibres in the dermis of those areas. For example, the skin around the eyes is thin and relatively mobile, compared to the thicker skin over the back.

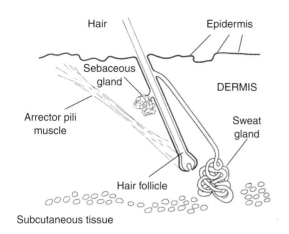

Hair

Epidermis

Sebaceous gland

DERMIS

Arrector pili muscle

Sweat gland

Hair follicle

Subcutaneous tissue

The dermis and epidermis (not to scale).

Hair Follicles

A single hair follicle can be thought of as a long, slender pit in the skin, which supports the hair. In the horse, each hair follicle contains only one hair. In comparison, the complex hair follicles of a dog have one long primary 'guard' hair and a number of shorter secondary 'undercoat' hairs. Each hair grows from a very metabolically active region at the base of the follicle. This region has a rich blood supply to bring in nutrients for, and remove waste products from, the intensely active growth process.

Hair follicles lie at a diagonal angle in the skin. The orientation of a follicle corresponds to the angle at which the hair leaves the skin and the direction in which the hair grows. Each hair follicle has a very small muscle, the **arrector pili muscle**, which can contract to raise the hair to a more vertical position. Horses in low environmental temperatures may raise their hair coat to trap a thicker layer of warm air next to the skin. We are familiar with this phenomenon as 'goosebumps' on our own skin when we are chilled. Goosebumps represent small raised areas of skin around individual erect hairs, and are readily visible in people as we are so sparsely haired.

Each hair follicle is accompanied by a **sweat gland**, which is located down in the dermis. Each gland has a duct, which carries sweat to the opening of the associated hair follicle. From there the sweat can move onto the skin surface. Horses sweat when their body temperature rises above a certain level. This may be a response to a high environmental temperature, to exercise or to having a fever. Sweating can also be seen with pain, stress, in horses with pituitary pars intermedia disease (PPID), or with a type of adrenal gland tumour (pheochromocytoma).

Each hair follicle has a **sebaceous gland**, which produces sebum. Sebum is an oily substance which passes along the sebaceous duct and into the hair follicle. It mixes with sweat and forms an emulsion on the surface of the skin. This oily and waxy layer contributes to the flexible, waterproof and antimicrobial character of the skin. It also coats the hair shafts, and gives them a glossy appearance and a pliable nature.

Hair

Even a single hair is a miracle of structural engineering. A hair is flexible, elastic, waterproof, strong and durable. Hair, like hoof and horn and nails, is made of a very stable and fibrous protein called keratin.

Each hair is a long cylinder with a pointed tip at one end and a root at the other. The cylinder is mostly made up of cortex, but also has an inner core (the medulla) and a thin outer cuticle. The medulla is relatively large in mane and tail hair. The elongated spindle-shaped cells of the cortex contain melanin granules, which determine the colour of the hair. The type and distribution of melanin granules are under genetic control and determine the colour of each hair. The cuticle is made of thin overlapping cells, arranged like a tiled roof, and with the exposed edges pointing towards the tip. At the base of the hair this textured surface pattern interlocks with the base of the hair follicle and holds the hair firmly in place.

Curly-coated horses, or 'curlies', have wavy or curly hair, particularly noticeable in the winter coat. The mane and tail also have a wavy or curly appearance. However, the hair follicles, and the parts of the hair inside the hair follicles, are as straight as in non-curly horses – the distinctive change in hair shape, to become curly, occurs after the hair leaves the body. Curly-coated horses can shed sections of their mane and tail at the time of coat shedding. These sections subsequently regrow.

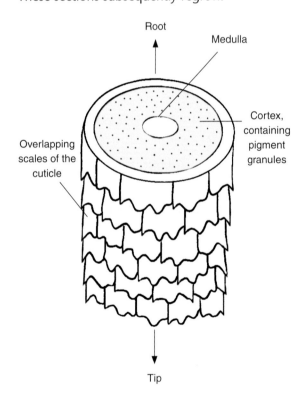

A section of a hair shaft.

The Hair Growth Cycle

The growth of body hair is cyclic, rather than continuous. There is a growing phase, which stops when the hair reaches the appropriate length. This is followed by a resting phase, when the hair is retained in the follicle before being shed. A growing hair is tightly attached at the active base of the follicle and is hard to pull out. Microscope examination of an epilated growing hair shows a fat, rounded, shiny root. The resting hair, by contrast, has a more slender, pointed, matt-textured root and is easy to pull out. Grooming, for example with a body brush, will dislodge some of the resting hairs that are ready to be shed.

Horses moult body hair in an ongoing mosaic pattern. This strategy helps to retain a functional hair covering over the body at any one time. Superimposed on this basic pattern there is usually major moulting activity, and hair replacement, at certain times of year. The timing of a major moult is mostly controlled by the length of day. To a lesser degree, it is influenced by the environmental temperature, genetic factors, quality of the diet, hormonal factors and general health. Mountain and moorland ponies, when living outside in the UK, have a major moult between the end of March and the end of May. Shedding of the winter coat starts at the legs and underneath the neck, and finishes over the back. This is a useful adaptive strategy in case of poor weather late in the year, as the back area gives significant protection. The fine summer coat is present for June, July and August, and the winter coat from September through to May. This pattern is closely adapted to the prevailing conditions in the UK, with only a short season of reliable summer weather in mountain and moorland areas.

The horse is born with a full complement of hair follicles. The foal coat has hairs that are very close together. This gives a dense 'fluffy' appearance, with the hairs more vertical and tightly packed than in the adult coat. The hair follicles become more widely spaced as the horse grows in size and the total area of skin increases.

A Welsh Mountain pony stallion in April, just starting to shed his winter coat.

The same Welsh Mountain pony stallion in July, in his summer coat. Note the change of coat colour between winter and summer coat, which is typical of a roan.

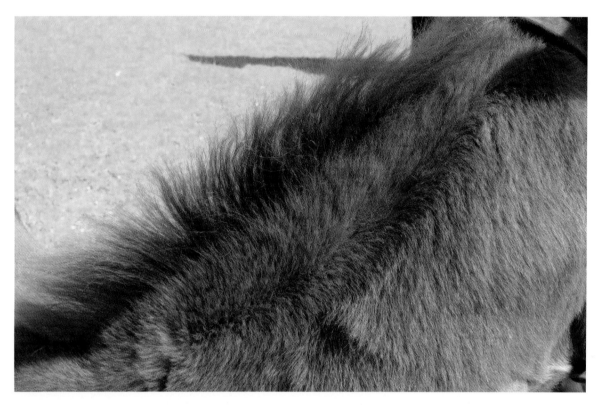

The dense, soft, fluffy coat of a foal. (Photo: D. Payani)

The Subcutaneous Layer

This layer has variable amounts of fat, depending on the body score of the individual horse. Large blood vessels run through the fat and connect with the smaller branching vessels of the dermis.

SKIN FUNCTION

The skin is the largest organ in the body and its proper functioning is crucial for life. The main role of the skin is as an external barrier and a protective envelope for the body. Skin cells and their surrounding material can be thought of as a tough, flexible, waterproof covering for the body. This covering keeps the outside out and the inside in.

Keeping the Outside Out

The large surface area of the skin comes into contact with a wide variety of different things – rain, grass, tack, flies, bedding, bacteria, etc. The skin is not just an inert or passive barrier; it is an immunologically active place. The skin's immune system has an important role in being tolerant of 'self', while recognizing and neutralizing 'other'. Sentinel cells of the immune system can detect characteristic features of viruses, bacteria, parasites, fungi and allergens in or on the skin. These sentinel cells communicate with the rest of the immune system to mobilize a response. The response is usually appropriate and protective but can, as in the case of the swelling and itching of allergic skin disease, cause problems of itself.

Protection from Ultraviolet Radiation

Ultraviolet radiation is potentially damaging to the skin. The amount of exposure to ultraviolet radiation depends on the horse's lifestyle and skin type, the time of year, the latitude and the local conditions. For example, a clipped horse with areas of white skin over the back and living in a sunny part of the world may escape radiation damage if he has access to, and chooses to use, a shade shelter when the sun is at its most intense. White or pink skin has an absence of the skin pigment, melanin. Melanin is able to absorb and dissipate most of the energy of ultraviolet radiation. It largely protects pigmented skin from radiation damage. The DNA contained in the cell nucleus is particularly vulnerable to radiation damage. Melanin pigment forms a dark-coloured protective cap over the nucleus of the cell.

The presence of hair physically blocks a significant amount of ultraviolet light from reaching the skin. Thinly haired areas, such as the muzzle or around the eyes, are more vulnerable to damage by ultraviolet radiation. Squamous cell carcinoma can develop in these areas, especially in horses with non-pigmented skin. There is a greater density of hair coat in areas routinely exposed to sunlight, such as over the back. The glossiness of a healthy hair coat will reflect away more sunlight than a dull coat.

Resilience and Flexibility

Skin cells fit and bind tightly together in overlapping layers. They are flexible and tough. These features, combined with the elasticity of deep skin layers and the cushioning of subcutaneous fat, allow the skin to withstand considerable physical pressure and shearing forces while simultaneously protecting underlying structures. The skin is thickest in areas likely to be exposed to damage, for example the outside of the legs and over the back. It is thinnest over the mobile eyelids and the relatively protected inside of the thighs. The elasticity and flexibility of the skin are readily appreciated over the knee, for example when a foreleg is lifted to pick out a hoof.

The outermost skin layers have flattened, resilient dead cells made of the strong structural protein called keratin. The cells are embedded in organized layers of lipids. The 'bricks and mortar' pattern resists physical and chemical damage, and provides waterproofing.

Waterproofing

Shedding of external water from the skin contributes to maintenance of the delicate and crucial water balance of the body. The direction in which the hair coat lies allows rain to be rapidly and efficiently shed from the body. The direction of hair growth varies over the body, with hairs forming 'streams' along which water can run. The body hair just in front of the hind legs points upwards and then outwards. This arrangement reduces the water flow down between the abdomen and the hind legs, and reduces wetting of the underbelly.

Traditionally coated mountain and moorland breeds have winter coats with a dense undercoat and a sparser top coat. The under-hairs are of a narrower diameter and form a soft springy 'wool' layer adjacent to the skin. This layer needs enough depth and resilience to resist being pushed flat onto the skin under the weight of windblown rain and wet top hair. The top hairs are thicker, more rigid and slightly longer. When rain falls on this type of coat the tips of groups of top hairs come together to form a triangle, with the tips pointing downwards. Water runs to the tips and flows or drops onto the adjacent triangle, and ultimately onto the ground, without running under the sparsely haired belly, or down past the dock. Long hairs down the sides of the cheeks allow water to drip off, rather than running under the jaw. The streams of hair under the neck meet

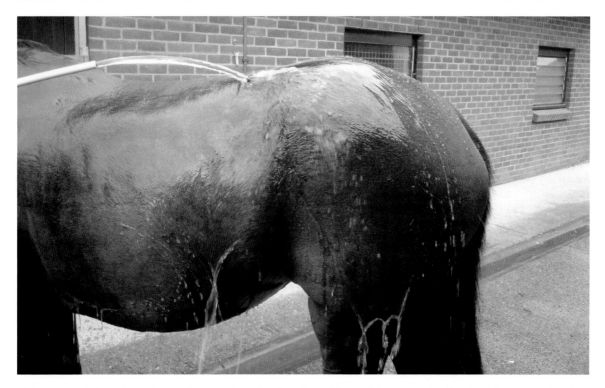

This horse is being hosed down after exercise. The direction of flow of the hair coat channels the water along with it. The upward-facing hairs in front of the hind leg deflect the water away. We can see that water is shed from the back, and the abdomen is kept relatively dry.

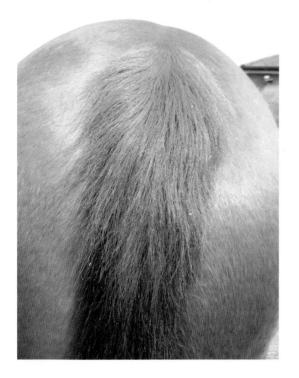

and point forwards, to reduce water flow under the chest. This system allows water to be rapidly and efficiently shed by channelling it over the top hair, while maintaining a warm dry layer of air next to the skin in the wool undercoat. The central hairs of the tail run straight down, but the shorter hairs near the base of the tail fan out to direct water onto adjacent body hairs and away from the dock.

The ability of the hair coat and skin to shed surface water can be overwhelmed by unusually prolonged and heavy rain, but this is unusual in a good-quality coat of a locally adapted native

Hairs of the tail. The central hairs point downward. The side hairs fan outward, to direct water away from the dock.

breed. Over-hydrated skin is more commonly seen after covering the skin for prolonged periods with insufficiently breathable materials, for example extended periods of occlusive bandaging.

Protection from Micro-organisms

The normal skin surface is not a sterile place. A healthy population of non-harmful micro-organisms occupies space on the skin. It also competes with harmful bacteria for available nutrients. The presence of non-harmful bacteria reduces the ability of a potentially harmful micro-organism to find a place to live, to multiply and to cause problems. The outer layer of the skin, the epidermis, is constantly producing cells at its base and shedding them at its outer edge. This progression of skin cells from deep to superficial layers, before being shed into the environment, represents a precarious foothold for pathogens trying to colonize the skin. It also allows the skin surface to be continually renewed and replaced. Other factors that make the skin surface a challenging environment for pathogens attempting to set up home are its dryness, the antimicrobial actions of sebum and sweat, the acidic pH, and the antimicrobial action of peptides, which are released from keratinocytes.

Healthy, intact skin maintains a low population of micro-organisms on its surface. Damaged skin, for example a wound or burn, will be rapidly colonized by bacteria, which may establish an infection.

Keeping the Inside In

Removing the skin of a dead animal does not cause the body to physically fall apart. From this, we know that the skin does not function just as a flexible box holding in the contents. However, horses with large areas of skin damage, for example burn patients after stable fires, face serious challenges to keep enough fluid, protein and electrolytes in the body, as well as keeping infection out.

Water Balance

The body of a horse is largely made of water, but the normal skin surface is a relatively dry place. This situation is achieved by a steeply decreasing gradient of water content from inside to outside, across the skin. The epidermal cells contain less fluid, and are surrounded by more lipid, towards the outside of the skin. This has the effect of reducing the loss of precious water, electrolytes and protein across the skin, and retaining them in the body.

A dehydrated horse will reduce the flow of blood to the skin and so prioritize the volume of blood pumped through the lungs, brain, heart, liver and kidneys. So-called 'tenting' of the skin is when a section is gently pulled, or pinched, up from the body and does not immediately spring back flat when released. This is usually done over the neck or shoulder. Tenting can be a sign of dehydration, but is unreliable as it can occur for other reasons. Older horses generally show skin tenting more easily than younger ones. The skin tent, or skin pinch test, does not correlate with blood test measures of dehydration and is not recommended. Assessing the dryness of a horse's mucous membranes is, unfortunately, similarly unreliable.

Temperature Regulation

The horse, as a typical mammal, regulates body temperature within a narrow range. The body contains many temperature-sensitive chemical reactions and enzyme systems. These systems are protected and promoted by close temperature regulation. The initial response to a change in temperature is usually behavioural. A horse will choose to move into the sun or shade, and stand in or out of the breeze. If these physical adaptations are not enough to maintain a comfortable temperature then physiological mechanisms, such as sweating or shivering, come into action. We are familiar with the free and generalized sweating of horses and people but, looking at mammals as a group, sweating is an unusual mechanism of thermoregulation.

Sweating

Horses have a well-developed ability to sweat. They are flight animals that respond to danger by bursts of intense muscular activity. Working muscles generate heat and horses need to get rid of excess body heat quickly and efficiently. Horse sweat contains water, protein and electrolytes such as sodium, calcium, magnesium, potassium and chloride. Fluid evaporates on the warm surface of the skin and has a cooling effect on the body. Sweating depletes the water reserves of the body and needs to be replaced by drinking. Some of the large internal reserve of water in the gut can be mobilized as a water source in the short term. A hot, sweating horse, without access to water, will become dehydrated over time. The rate of sweating depends on the ambient temperature and humidity, and the movement of air currents around the skin. A sweating horse can lose 10 litres (17.6 pints) of fluid in an hour of exercise.

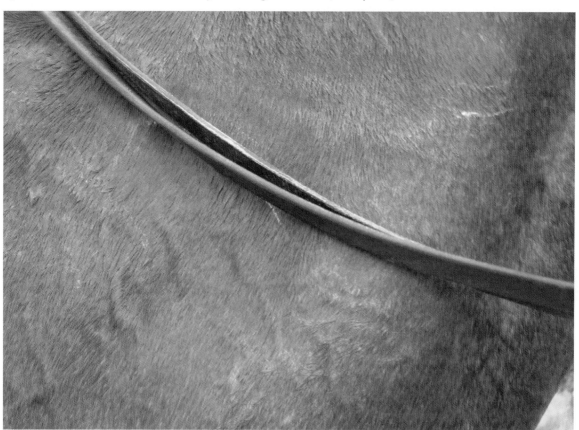

A sweating polo pony, at the end of a chukka. The veins near the surface of the skin are dilated to dissipate heat. Lines of white lather can be seen on the reins and the skin. The skin and hair coat are wet with sweat.

EVAPORATION

Evaporation occurs when some water molecules have enough heat energy to move from the surface of a liquid into the adjacent air. It can happen when the liquid (the horse's sweat) has enough heat energy, and when the adjacent air is not already saturated with water. Air movement, for example a breeze across the skin, moves saturated air away and speeds the rate of evaporation. Water molecules move from the surface of a liquid so the larger that surface – for example skin and hairs coated in sweat – the greater the rate of evaporation. Why does the evaporation of sweat cool the horse? When the more energetic water molecules leave the skin surface they take heat energy with them, and leave behind a lower-energy and cooler situation. Sweating provides a mechanism for transferring body heat into the environment.

Compared to human sweat, horse sweat contains more protein and less salt (sodium chloride). The dominant sweat protein is latherin, which acts as a surfactant (a surface active agent). Sweat needs to pass from the skin surface, and through the waterproof hairy layer, to evaporate. It is thought that the surfactant properties of latherin allow sweat to more effectively wet the skin surface and the hair coat, so promoting evaporation and heat loss from a larger surface area.

Sweat is produced by coiled sweat glands in the lower part of the dermis. It travels from the gland, towards the skin surface, through a duct. The duct opens into the hair follicle, just down from the skin surface. Sweat glands occur all over the body and have their highest density between the lower jaws, around the lips and eyes, the coronets and mane. Sweating is controlled by hormones, such as adrenalin, released from the adrenal glands, or by nerves acting on the sweat glands. Horses can sweat in response to pain, exercise, low blood sugar, a warm environment, excitement, stress and certain medical conditions such as pituitary pars intermedia dysfunction (PPID).

Action of the Blood Vessels

Blood vessels in the skin open wider in warm ambient temperatures. This brings larger amounts of warm blood to the skin surface and facilitates heat loss from the body by convection, conduction and radiation. In cold temperatures blood circulation to the skin is restricted to the minimum, so conserving body heat. Arteries carry oxygenated, nutrient-rich blood to the skin. Veins carry oxygen-depleted blood, and waste products, away from the skin. In between the arteries and veins is a detailed network of vessels for supply and drainage. This complex web of thin-walled blood vessels is called a capillary bed. In cold conditions these capillary beds can be largely bypassed by the widening of shunts or connections, which connect arteries directly to veins.

The large blood vessels of the skin run through the subcutaneous layer. In this location they are protected, insulated and cushioned by surrounding fat.

Insulation

The subcutaneous layer contains stored fat. This deposit of fat varies in thickness with the region of the body and the condition of the animal. As well as being a store of future energy for the horse, the fat layer provides physical insulation against temperature changes. Horses with too much body fat typically have a prominent, solid crest, a rounded 'apple-shaped' bottom, and ribs that cannot be easily felt through the skin.

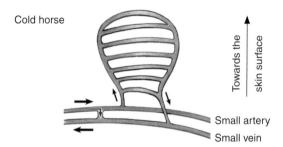

Warm horse

Network of small blood vessels in the dermis

Small artery

Small vein

Shunt is closed. A lot of blood circulates close to the skin surface and contributes to heat loss

Cold horse

Towards the skin surface

Small artery

Small vein

Shunt between artery and vein is open. Blood takes path of least resistance. Circulation to outer part of skin is minimal.

The shunt mechanism between an artery and a vein in the skin. When the horse is hot, the shunt has a small diameter. Blood moves from the artery and around the network of small vessels, which are close to the skin surface. Body heat is transferred, via the bloodstream, to the outer cooler regions of the horse and is lost to the environment. When the horse is cold, the shunt has a large diameter. A lot of the blood runs from the artery through the shunt and into the vein, without travelling through the network of small vessels. This diverts blood from the cool outer parts of the skin and conserves more of the horse's body heat.

Different horses carry fat in different areas. It is helpful to assess a number of body areas before coming to an overall fat score. A 1 to 5 scoring system is simple and useful, with 1 being very thin, 2 underweight, 3 correct weight, 4 overweight, and 5 very fat. In recent times

RADIATION, CONVECTION AND CONDUCTION

Radiation of heat occurs via electromagnetic waves. For example, a horse standing in warm sunshine will be receiving electromagnetic radiation that has been emitted by the sun, and has travelled through space, before reaching the skin.

Heat loss by **convection** involves movement and flow. For example, heat will rise from a horse standing in a field on a cold day. As the warm air rises away from the skin, colder air will be drawn in to take its place. A rug would trap a layer of warm air around the body and reduce convective heat loss.

Conduction requires contact with the skin, for example a horse standing in cool water will lose heat to the water. A horse leaning against a warm wall will gain heat from the wall. The most important factors affecting heat gain or loss are the surface area of skin in contact and the temperature difference between the skin and the other surface.

increasing numbers of horses in the Western world have a body score of 4 or 5.

Efficient heat insulation can be seen when snow rests on a pony's back for a prolonged period, just as snow will sit for long spells on a well-insulated roof. The natural winter coat has a dense, wool-like undercoat which traps a layer of warm air close to the skin. The hair coat is sufficiently waterproof and incompressible to retain the dry warm air layer under the weight of snow. As mentioned earlier, changes in hair density and length are seen through the seasons of the year. Native ponies living outside in the UK will carry an effective winter coat from September to May.

This horse is underweight. The overall appearance is angular. The withers and croup are prominent. The neck is thin and the ribs are easy to see. (Photo: World Horse Welfare)

This horse is overweight. The overall appearance is rounded. The outline of the withers is lost. The croup is rounded. The neck is thick, with a fat-filled crest. The ribs cannot be seen or felt. (Photo: World Horse Welfare)

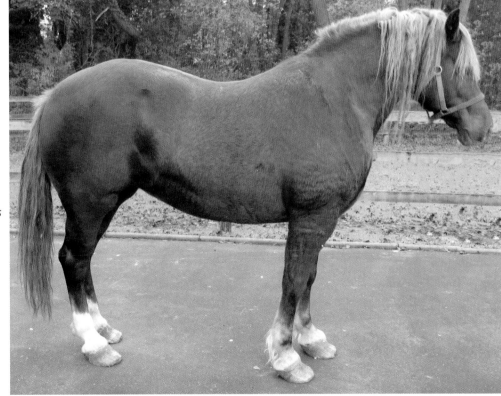

Horses kept inside, or rugged up through colder months, may have altered moult cycles and coat types. The coat type and moult cycle will depend on the horse's experience of day length and ambient temperature, as well as on individual genetic, nutritional and health factors. The thermal efficiency of a hair coat can be influenced by bathing, grooming and clipping.

A dark coat colour is likely to absorb more energy from the sun's rays than a pale one.

Donkeys are Special

Donkeys are able to tolerate higher environmental temperatures than horses. In common with camels, they are adapted to live in warm, dry parts of the world. Donkeys can allow their body temperature to drift over a wider temperature range than horses. A donkey's relatively long coat shades the skin from sunlight and provides some insulation against high ambient temperatures. The pale hair colour reflects ultraviolet radiation away from the skin. The melanin pigment, in the darkly coloured skin, absorbs and dissipates some of the energy of the ultraviolet radiation.

Other Functions of the Skin

Sensing the Environment

There is a complex network of nerves in the skin. Nerves specialize in different tasks and have specialized endings for the job. Some nerves send messages, while others receive and transmit information. They are able to sense pain, pressure, itch, heat and cold. We readily think of a horse using his eyes and ears in sensing the environment around him, but the skin also has an important protective role and is the largest sensory organ in the body. It allows the horse to receive detailed information about

the world around him, such as wind speed and direction, contact by insects, plant texture and the heat of the sun.

The panniculus is a large, but thin, cloak of muscle covering the upper legs and the trunk. When the horse senses something touching the skin, contraction of the nearest section of the panniculus muscle causes that part of the skin to shudder or twitch. We can see the panniculus muscle in action when a fly tries repeatedly to land on the trunk, or the upper legs, and is dislodged by the sharp movement of the skin. The panniculus does not extend to the lower legs, head or neck. Standing head to tail with another horse can give fly protection for heads and necks, by the mutual swishing of tails.

Sensory hairs occur around the muzzle, eyes and ears. They are sometimes known as tactile hairs. They are long, thick, stiff, single hairs which emerge from large hair follicles. Sensory hairs have a good supply of nerves around their base. They are very sensitive to being touched or moved, and their roots are located deeper in the skin than normal hairs. They probably have a protective function

Long, stiff, sensory hairs around the eye.

for the important, exposed and vulnerable structures of the head.

Vitamin D Production

Vitamin D3 is made in the skin by the action of sunlight on vitamin D precursor molecules. Synthesis takes place in the deeper layers of the epidermis.

In most mammals, vitamin D has a vital role in the uptake, and the metabolism, of calcium and phosphate. By contrast, vitamin D does not seem to have this role in the horse. The levels of vitamin D found in the blood of horses are much lower than in other mammals that have been studied. Vitamin D is found in dried forage, such as meadow hay and alfalfa.

Specialized Areas of Skin

The hoof, frog, sole, ergots and chestnuts are specialized areas of skin.

The hoof, frog and sole are important components of the horse's foot. They are composed of different types of keratin compared to those found in other areas of the skin.

Hoof

The hoof is a tough protective layer for the foot. It is made of specialized skin and a particularly resilient type of keratin. The actively dividing cells which form the hoof wall are in the basal layer of the coronary band. The coronary band has a rich blood supply to support the metabolically active process of producing the hoof wall: we know that a wound to the coronary band can bleed profusely. The hoof is formed of parallel keratin tubules, and inter-tubular horn, which grow down from the coronary band. They grow at a rate of approximately 1cm (0.4in) per month. Damage to the coronary band may, in the long term, result in a defect that runs all the way down the hoof wall. The hoof wall, like the epidermis of the skin, contains no nerves or blood vessels. This allows it to have a hot metal shoe pushed against it, and nails driven into it to hold the shoe in place.

A recently shod foot, showing the hoof wall.

Hoof colour is determined by the activity of melanocytes in the coronary band. Active melanocytes in the basal layer of the coronary band will produce melanin pigment and the hoof will be black. Hooves can be black, white or vertically striped, to reflect the activity of the melanocytes. The colour of the hoof tends to match the colour of the adjacent skin and hair coat.

Frog

The frog fills the back part of the base of the hoof. It has a triangular shape and grows down in layers from the bottom of the foot towards the ground. The keratin that makes up the frog is softer than that of the hoof wall or the sole. The softer and more elastic nature of the frog contributes to shock absorption, and protects the underlying flexor tendon.

The frog can feel particularly soft and rubbery if the horse has been in damp conditions underfoot. The surface can also dry out, in dry conditions, and feel much harder. The surface layers of the frog are shed in irregular chunks.

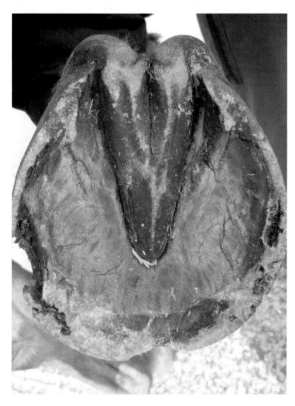

The triangular frog and the surrounding sole cover the base of the foot.

Sole

The sole covers the rest of the bottom of the foot. Like the frog, the sole grows in layers from the base of the foot towards the ground. Ideally, the rate at which the layers are shed is matched by the rate of cell production, to give a constant thickness of sole. The sole needs to be tough and thick enough to protect the foot from sharp stones. It also needs to be flexible and thin enough to change shape as the hoof wall expands and contracts.

Ergots and Chestnuts

These horny skin projections are thought to be remnants of the very different structure of the ancestral horse's leg. The ancestral horse, *Eohippus*, was thought to have walked on five toes. The fossil record shows a progressive reduction in the number of functional toes over time. The current horse – *Equus caballus* – takes all of the bodyweight on one central toe. Ergots and chestnuts are thought to be the vestigial remains of the shortened extra toes.

Chestnuts are usually found on all four legs, but are more prominent on the forelegs. They are found on the inside of the leg, above the knee on the forelegs and below the hock on the hind legs. They grow with time and the top horny layers are naturally shed from the surface. Horses will sometimes bite at them and peel layers away. They can be trimmed or peeled

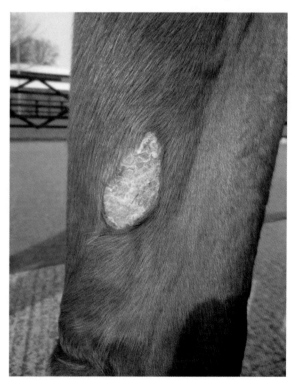

A horny chestnut, on the inside of a foreleg.

for cosmetic reasons, and softened with hoof oil or petroleum jelly. The cross-section of a chestnut may be pointed, round, oval or pear-shaped. While the thickness increases with time, the cross-sectional shape is constant over the horse's lifespan. The shape of chestnuts can be used as an identification feature in horses with few other distinctive marks.

Ergots are approximately the same size on all four legs. They occur at the back of the fetlock and, owing to the surrounding hair, are often easier to feel than to see. They vary in size between individuals, from negligible to very prominent.

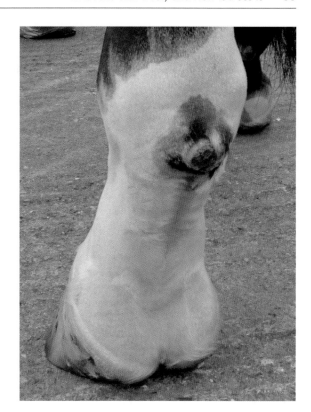

This horny ergot, at the back of the fetlock, is only visible because the hair which normally covers it (the 'foot lock') has been clipped away.

3 Identifying Individual Horses by Sight

Some horses can be individually identified by their distinctive coat colour, for example the unique distribution of black and white haired areas on a piebald horse. Other horses will have a more uniform and prevalent coat colour, such as bay, and will need additional unique features to identify them. These additional features include whorls, white markings and flesh markings. Both the coat colour and the location of additional distinctive features are routinely marked on the diagram of a horse's passport.

GENETICS AND COAT COLOUR

Horses can have a very wide variety of different coat colours and markings. Certain breeds, with their limited gene pools, have only one or a few restricted coat colours. For example, the Suffolk horse always has a chestnut coat, mane and tail. (For this breed, the old spelling 'chesnut' is retained.)

An Introduction to Genetics

Many characteristics of an individual horse, including the colour of the skin and the hair coat, are inherited from the parents. The dam and sire, in turn, will have inherited their characteristics from their parents. The recipe for each of these heritable characteristics is written in code and passed down the generations. An egg inside a mare and a sperm from a stallion each contain only one half of a set of genetic

WHORLS

Whorls are distinctive changes of coat direction. The number, location and type of whorls vary between horses, but they are permanent features of an individual. They are important in identifying individual horses.

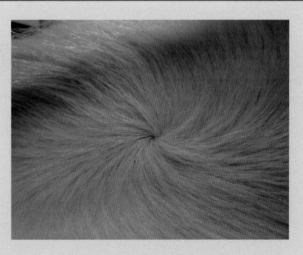

Whorls are where the hair coat changes direction. In this simple whorl, on the neck, the hair radiates out from a central point and lies in a counterclockwise direction.

Suffolk horses in a mare and foal class at the Suffolk Show. They are all chesnut in colour. They have no white facial markings, other than a possible white star. The Suffolk horse is listed as a critically rare breed.

material. When the egg and sperm come together at mating the two halves combine and form the whole genetic make-up of the new foal. The foal is similar to his dam, as he has half of the genetic recipe from her. The foal is also different from his dam, as he has half of his genetic code from the sire. The way in which the two halves of the genetic material combine makes each individual unique. Even when the same mating is repeated, subsequent foals will not be exactly the same.

Genes contain long tracts of coded information, some of which are translated inside the developing foal into a functional reality. Genes determine a myriad of bodily functions, but also such readily appreciated features as the structural appearance of the body, and colour of the coat. Dominant genes will have their information expressed in preference to recessive ones.

Types of gene (genotypes) can be written down to show what an individual has inherited from the parents. The dominant type of gene is conventionally written with a capital letter, and the recessive type with a lower case letter.

SOME TERMS USED IN GENETICS

DNA is an abbreviation for **d**eoxyribo**n**ucleic **a**cid. DNA is tightly packed into chromosomes and contains the linear coded information for passing on hereditary characteristics to the next generation.

A **chromosome** is a package of DNA. Each chromosome contains a large number of genes. A horse has sixty-four chromosomes and a donkey sixty-two. The chromosomes are arranged in pairs. One chromosome in each pair comes from the sire, the other chromosome comes from the dam. A mule has sixty-three chromosomes. This uneven number is associated with a mule not, usually, being able to breed.

A **gene** is a specific section of DNA, on a chromosome, which is responsible for coding for a certain heritable characteristic. Only a small number of genes are responsible for determining the coat colour of a horse.

The **genotype** is the genetic make-up of an individual.

How Coat Colours are Determined

Black and Chestnut

The colour of a horse's hair coat is determined by a small number of genes. There are two basic coat colours: black and chestnut. These two colours relate to the two pigment colours made in the skin. Horses with the type of gene E/E produce the black pigment eumelanin, and have black pigment in their hair. E is the dominant gene, so horses with the genetic make-up (genotype) E/e are also black, or of a related colour. Horses with the genotype e/e produce the reddish pigment pheomelanin. They have this red-brown pigment in the hairs and have a chestnut coat colour. If we mixed together black and chestnut paint colours we would get a dark colour that was neither black nor chestnut. This does not happen with black and chestnut horses as the colour is either dominant or recessive, and comes out as a true colour, not as a mixture.

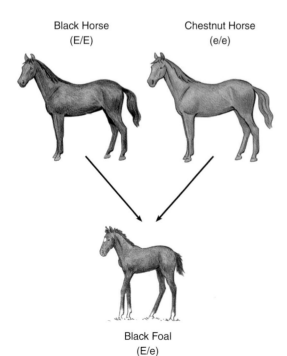

Black Horse
(E/E)

Chestnut Horse
(e/e)

Black Foal
(E/e)

A diagram of a black horse (E/E) mated with a chestnut horse (e/e), and producing a black foal. The foal inherits one version of the gene from each parent and will have the genotype E/e. Because E is a dominant gene the foal will have a coat colour which is black, or will be in the black coat colour family. The foal has inherited the dominant E gene, so the outcome of this mating cannot be a chestnut foal.

A smartly turned out black Welsh section D cross, in harness. This gelding will have the genotype E/E or E/e.

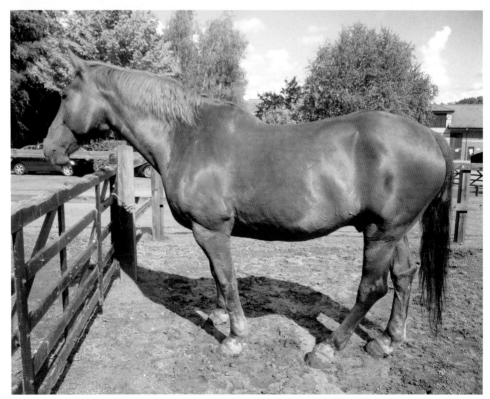

A chestnut gelding standing in the sunshine. This horse will have the genotype e/e.

When the E/e, E/E or e/e genotypes are present, without the action of other genes, horses will be black (E/e or E/E) or chestnut (e/e). Horses will have other coat colours, apart from black or chestnut, when a variety of other genes are present to modify the basic outcome. Modifications of black can produce colours such as bay, buckskin, blue roan, seal brown, and bay dun. Modifications of the basic chestnut colour can result in, for example, palomino, cremello, red roan and red dun. We can see that coat colours tend to fall into a black coat colour family, or a chestnut coat colour family.

Bay

Bay is a very common coat colour produced by a combination of genes. Bay horses have a chestnut (brown) body and black 'points'. They are capable of producing black pigment so they have a basic E/E or E/e genotype, and are in the black family of coat colours. The black hair coloration is restricted to the mane and tail, the edges or tips of the ears, and the legs, particularly the lower legs.

This restriction of black is caused by the presence of the agouti gene. When the agouti gene is dominant (A/A or A/a genotype) the

A dark bay Welsh section C, in hand. Bays can have different degrees of colour dilution in the body hair, varying from pale chestnut through to dark brown. The mane and tail and lower legs are black. Dark bays may be more likely to have the genotype E/E.

Black edges to the ears are a variable feature of the bay colour.

horse will be bay. With the recessive a/a gene there is no restriction effect and the horse can be black over the whole body.

Dun

Dun is an interesting colour, or more descriptively a dilution of another colour. We saw with the undiluted black and chestnut colours the action of dominant and recessive genes giving one colour or the other. In contrast to this, the dominant dun gene (D/D and D/d) has an equal dilution effect on both the black and the red hair pigments. It dilutes the intensity of the base colour over the neck and the trunk. When the dun gene acts on the basic black coat type the horse may be bay

dun. Dilution of the basic chestnut coat colour will produce a red dun. The mane and tail, the dorsal stripe and the legs remain the underlying undiluted base colour.

Some dun horses show stripes of dark hair at the back of the forelegs, and across the shoulders. They may also have a paler colour to some of the outside hairs of the mane and tail. Dun coloration is a feature of the primitive Przewalski's horse and is thought to be one of the oldest coat colour types. Horses in prehistoric cave paintings have a recognizable dun coat type. The colour of the eyes and the colour of the skin are unaffected by the dun gene. Horses with the recessive dun gene (d/d) will have undiluted, strongly pigmented hair coats and no features of the dun coloration.

A Konik pony, native to Poland, with the dun coloration typical of the breed. There is a dark dorsal stripe, mane and tail. The face and lower legs are darker than the body. This pony will have the basic E/E or E/e genotype to give black, plus the dominant D/D or D/d dun genotype, which dilutes the black colour over the body to dun. Several herds of Konik ponies are used in the management of nature reserves in the UK. The ponies are placid around people, hardy, and suitable for rough grazing.

Palomino

Palomino is in the chestnut family group of coat colours. To have the palomino colour a horse needs the basic chestnut genotype e/e, plus a single dose of dilution from the cream gene (N/Cr).The reddish chestnut colour of the hair coat is diluted to gold. The mane and tail are diluted to a greater degree than the hair coat and are almost white. The cream gene affects the eyes and the skin, as well as the hair coat colour. The cream gene can give different degrees of colour dilution, resulting in the various shades of palomino coat that occur. A true palomino is genetically different from a chestnut horse with a flaxen mane and tail. The chestnut does not carry the cream gene.

Buckskin

A buckskin horse, in common with a palomino, has one copy of the cream gene (N/Cr). Unlike the palomino, which has the basic chestnut genotype, a buckskin has a bay genotype and is in the black coloration family. The single dose of cream dilution is acting on the underlying bay colour. A bay horse is black (E), plus agouti restriction of black to the points (A). The outcome of cream dilution on bay is a distinctive pale golden or tan coloured coat with a black mane, tail and lower legs. The buckskin colour is sometimes confused with dun. Buckskins do not show any of the 'primitive' coat markings of the dun, including the dark dorsal stripe.

The colour palomino is a dilution of chestnut. This gelding will have the e/e chestnut genotype, plus a single dose of the cream gene (N/Cr). Palominos can have different degrees of colour dilution in the body hair, varying from very pale to dark gold. The mane and tail are always fully diluted to near white. (Photo: S. Goodall)

A buckskin champion. Buckskin is a dilution of bay. Like palomino, the buckskin has a single dose of the cream gene (N/Cr); unlike palomino, the buckskin is in the black family of coat colours. (Photo: T. Wigren)

Grey

We tend to think of grey as a separate coat colour, when it is really a dilution of other coat colours. The greying gene causes horses to turn grey, usually with a progressively lighter shade over time. The skin and eye pigmentation remain the same, usually of a dark colour.

ABOVE: The same grey mare at eight years of age. Note that the head is often the first place to lighten in colour. (Photo: K. Felton)

ABOVE: Grey mare at five years of age. The dominant greying gene (G/G or G/g) dilutes the underlying coat colour to grey. It causes the hairs to turn progressively lighter with age. (Photo: K. Felton)

BELOW: The same grey mare at thirteen years of age. The greying gene is linked to an increased risk of melanoma. This mare was euthanized at fourteen years of age because of complications with melanoma. (Photo: K. Felton)

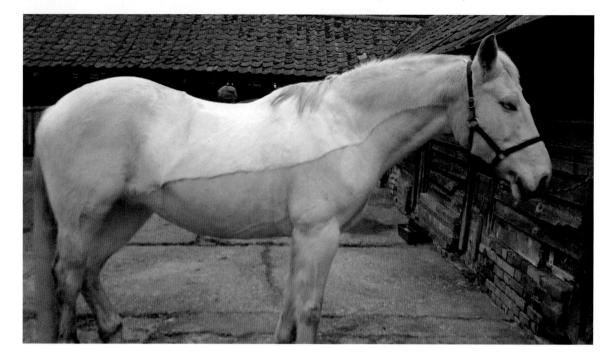

This type of greying is a dominant trait and has a G/G or G/g genotype. Grey horses can have any base coat colour, visible when they are born. For example, adult Lippizaners are mostly grey but foals are born bay or black. The dominant greying gene will dilute any other coat colour. Horses with the recessive genotype (g/g) will remain a consistent coat colour over their lifetime. They will not be grey. The greying gene carries with it an increased risk of developing the skin cancer melanoma, and the cosmetic condition vitiligo.

White

A truly white horse has both white hair and a pale-pink skin. This is a very unusual colour and is associated with the white gene (W). Older grey horses may have a lot of hair that has turned white but their skin colour, underneath the white hair, is dark.

Roan

The roan coloration is created by a mixture of white and coloured hairs over the trunk and neck. The hair coat of the legs furthest from the body, the head, the mane and the tail all have a darker colour, with relatively few white hairs mixed in. Roan is a dominant gene, so roan horses will have the genotype Rn/Rn or Rn/rn.

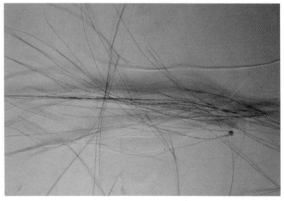

A group of hairs pulled from the shoulder area of a strawberry (red) roan horse. Roan horses have a mixture of coloured and white hairs over the body. Against a white background the chestnut hairs are most visible.

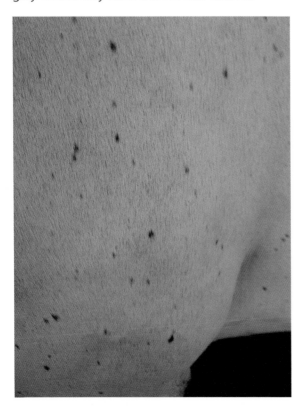

Close up of the coat of a fourteen-year-old 'flea bitten' grey gelding. The coat is pale grey/white with frequent discrete spots of chestnut.

The same group of hairs against a brown background. The white hairs are now more visible than the chestnut ones.

The appearance of roan horses varies with the amount of white hairs intermixed in the coat, and with the base coat colour. For example, a black base colour plus the roan gene gives a blue roan. A chestnut base colour, plus the roan gene, gives a strawberry (red) roan. Damage to the skin of a roan horse usually results in a patch of hair regrowth that has only the dark base colour, and not the intermixed white. The body colour of roan horses generally looks paler with the summer coat than with the winter coat.

What is a Coloured Horse?

Horses with large, well-defined areas of both white and another coat colour are referred to as coloured horses.

Piebald horses have large patches of black and white coloured hair over the body. They are capable of producing black pigment so they have a basic E/E or E/e genotype, and are in the black family of coat colours. The white areas have an absence of melanocytes, and are unable to manufacture pigment for the skin or hairs. When a piebald horse is clipped to the skin, the patches of black and white hair exactly match the patches of pigmented and non-pigmented skin.

Skewbald horses have large patches of any colour, other than black, and white hair. In reality a skewbald is generally brown and white, as bay and chestnut are the commonest non-black colours.

A strawberry (red) roan Shetland pony.

Tobiano One form of coloured pattern, tobiano, is associated with a known gene. The gene for being tobiano is dominant, so horses with a tobiano pattern will have the genotype TO/TO, or TO/to. Tobiano horses generally have the darker colour on the head, and are white on the lower legs. The white body patches generally have rounded margins.

WHITE MARKINGS

White Markings Present from Birth

Horses can have a wide range of white markings. They occur most commonly on the head and legs, but may be a feature of any part of the body. The shape and extent of the white markings with which a foal is born are determined by a number of genes. White markings usually have underlying non-pigmented skin, but may have a border of dark-coloured skin. The colour pattern of the underlying skin may only be obvious when the white-haired area is clipped for surgery, or when the skin is wet. White markings are very useful features by which to identify individual horses, and are marked on the diagram in a horse's passport. White markings have been disguised over the years to pass off one horse as another, both in the film industry when multiple horses are used for the same role, and for less genuine purposes.

The handsome coloured middleweight hunter stallion, Stormhill Mink. (Photo: R. Walker)

White facial markings can vary in extent from only a small white snip on the nose, to an entirely white face. The markings have familiar names, sometimes several names. The same marking, in different parts of the world, may have a different familiar name. A star is a white patch on the forehead, between the eyes. A blaze is a broad band of white hair running down the centre of the face. A blaze extends from the forehead to, usually, the muzzle. A snip is a small white patch on the nose, between the nostrils. A stripe is a narrow band of white hair running down the centre of the

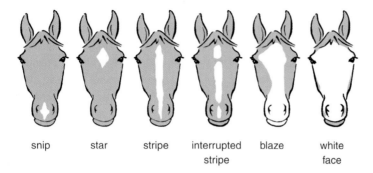

| snip | star | stripe | interrupted stripe | blaze | white face |

Examples of white facial markings.

All of these inquisitive faces have different and distinctive white markings.

face. It may be continuous or interrupted, and may merge with a star.

White leg markings may feature on one, two, three or all four legs of an individual horse – or there may be no legs carrying a white marking. The markings, when present, vary in extent from a few white hairs at the coronet to a full white leg extending up to the stifle area of a hind leg. High white markings usually extend higher on the hind legs than on the forelimbs in solid coloured horses.

White body markings are much less common at birth, in the general horse population, than white facial or leg markings. They are a feature of certain breeds, such as the Shire horse.

Acquired White Markings

Some white markings are acquired later in life – that is, the horse was not born with them.

FLESH MARKINGS

Flesh markings are patches of unpigmented skin. They are visible on thinly haired areas such as the lips and around the eyes.

The melanoctyes (pigment-producing cells) are very sensitive to skin damage. They can be affected by different types of skin damage, for example by hot or cold branding, wounds and inflammation. Radiation therapy and pressure sores commonly result in acquired white markings. The skin damage affects the melanocytes, but does not affect the ability of the hair to grow. This results in white hairs at the site of the damage. In freeze-branding the melanocytes are intentionally damaged by contact with a low temperature. The melanocytes are more sensitive to cold than the other cell types in the skin, and the hair

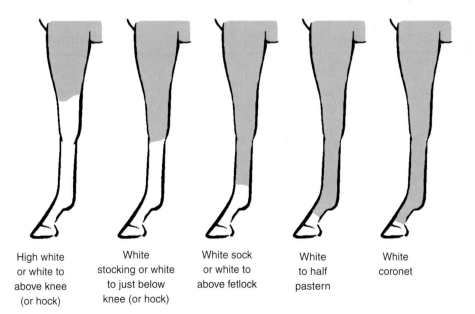

| High white or white to above knee (or hock) | White stocking or white to just below knee (or hock) | White sock or white to above fetlock | White to half pastern | White coronet |

Examples of white leg markings.

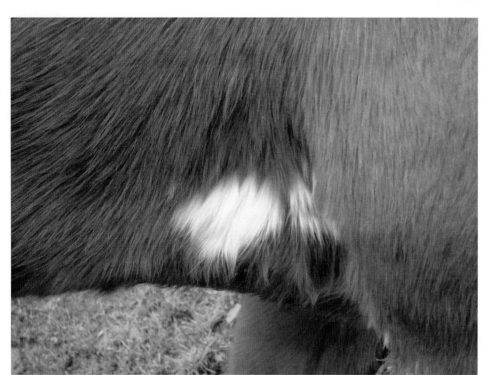

Acquired white markings at the site of pressure sores caused by a poorly fitting girth.

consequently regrows without pigment in the branded areas. If the branding device is left on the skin for too long, other skin cells may be damaged and the area may be scarred and hairless.

Vitiligo is a condition in which horses acquire white-haired spots and patches. The loss of pigment can occur at any age, but it is mostly seen in youngstock. The white markings are most often seen around the eyes, muzzle and lips. They can also occur on the perineum, or on a single body area such as the neck or chest. The underlying skin may or may not also lose its pigment. Arabian horses have a relatively high incidence of vitiligo. It has also been referred to as Arabian fading syndrome, or Arabian pinky syndrome, within the breed. The role of inherited genes, and of antibodies directed against the skin's pigment-producing cells, is as yet unclear. Vitiligo may resolve spontaneously, and in some horses the condition waxes and wanes over time. Although vitiligo is visually striking, it is only a cosmetic condition. However, loss of pigment around the eyes carries the risk of skin damage from ultraviolet radiation. Sun protection measures are sensible in such cases to help avoid sunburn and/or squamous cell carcinoma.

4 Gathering the Information

The great advantage of skin abnormalities, compared to those of internal organs, is that they can readily be seen and felt. A lot of useful information can be gathered without expensive equipment or special circumstances. We need good light, a co-operative animal, time, patience, and a thorough familiarity with what is normal. The horse is a large animal, with a lot of skin area, so having a pattern for systematic examination will help us to see all of the important changes and not to miss anything. Paying attention to the skin while grooming can provide horse-keepers with a regular opportunity to look for any changes in the quality or architecture of the skin or coat. It is helpful to look at the skin with curious attention and an open mind, in order to notice and understand what may be occurring.

TAKING A HISTORY

Skin disease is often diagnosed through taking a thorough history. The long list of possible causes can usually be whittled down to a shorter list when we understand the initial signs, and the progression of the disease. The horse's diet, the seasonality of the signs, possible skin lesions on in-contact people, and the state of any in-contact horses, can all be important. Is the horse itchy? Does the horse have pain? Information can also be reviewed on other medical problems, any drug history, the management routine, and the response to previous skin treatments. The age, the occupation, the breed, and the body score of the horse can also be relevant to their skin disease. A good history depends on attentive listening and asking the right questions, as well as on the accuracy and reliability of the information given. Using a history sheet can be helpful as a checklist, to ensure that information is not missed during a conversation with the owner or handler. History sheets can also be adapted and sent out, as a questionnaire to the owner/keeper, before a consultation.

The initial appearance of a skin disease often gives the best information for a diagnosis. The first time we look at the skin, these helpful early lesions may be old and resolving, or secondarily infected, or traumatized by rubbing on a fence post. Ongoing skin conditions are likely to produce, at some stage, a new crop of fresh lesions. The observant handler can then take photographs, make notes and alert the vet to the recurrence.

Keeping Records

Our memories can be unreliable. It is useful to note down the size, the shape and the appearance of skin lesions, along with the observation date. Photographs can also be helpful, especially when incorporating a sense

Name of owner and horse ————————————————————

Today's date ————————————————————

Age, breed, sex, and use of horse ————————————————————

Length of time with current owner ————————————————————

Any history from previous owner(s) ————————————————————

Medical history (other than skin) ————————————————————

Drug history ————————————————————

Travel history ————————————————————

Worming programme ————————————————————

Insect control ————————————————————

Diet, including supplements ————————————————————

Management pattern (grazing, stabling, rugs, etc.) ————————————

· ·

Main concern about the skin ————————————————————

When first noticed? ————————————————————

Where on skin first noticed? ————————————————————

What did it first look like? ————————————————————

Has it spread or changed? ————————————————————

Has it been there since started, or gone and returned? ——————————

Is there a seasonal pattern? ————————————————————

Is the horse itchy? Or painful? ————————————————————

Type, and frequency, of behaviours displayed? ——————————————

Are related horses affected? ————————————————————

Are in-contact horses affected? ————————————————————

Are in-contact people affected? ————————————————————

Any response to previous treatments? ——————————————————

Any change in skin with changes of environment? ————————————

Additional information ————————————————————

————————————————————————————————————

————————————————————————————————————

————————————————————————————————————

————————————————————————————————————

————————————————————————————————————

CASE NO.   **DATE**

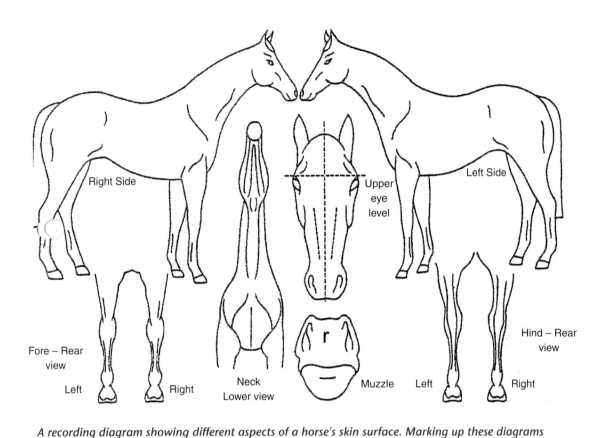

Right Side

Left Side

Upper
eye
level

Fore – Rear
view

Hind – Rear
view

Left   Right

Neck
Lower view

r

Muzzle   Left   Right

A recording diagram showing different aspects of a horse's skin surface. Marking up these diagrams with the size, shape and appearance of skin lesions forms part of a useful record. They are used, in combination with dates, photographs and written notes, to follow the development of lesions over time.

_____

_____

_____

_____

_____

_____

of scale alongside the lesion. A ruler or a coin can be a useful reference point in a photograph, but a hand or a finger works if nothing else is readily available. Looking back at previous dated photographs can be helpful to remind us of how things have changed.

We use a combination of digital photographs and paper recording sheets in the clinic to record the appearance of skin lesions on any one day. These details are very helpful in assessing the future progression of disease, and the response to treatment.

EXAMINING THE HORSE

Initial Overview

It is important to examine the skin in good-quality natural light. Simply examining a horse outdoors, rather than inside a dark building, can make a significant difference. Natural light usually gives a better idea of colour than an equivalent intensity of artificial light. Another reason for looking at the horse outside is the need to look from a distance. It is helpful to walk around the horse and get a general impression of his appearance, demeanour and general health before focusing in. A distant view also allows the overall pattern and distribution of obvious skin lesions to be seen. Looking at the detail and the main concerns last is a useful technique to ensure that nothing is missed. It allows the main concerns to be seen in the context of this individual horse in this particular environment.

Even a small pony has a large area of skin. It takes time, patience and a systematic approach to look at the skin properly, especially if it is necessary to part a long, shaggy coat to see it. Looking at more than the obviously affected areas allows us to understand what is normal for that individual. It also allows us to spot less obvious lesions, which we would otherwise have missed.

Under the Microscope

A clean microscope, with good-quality optics, is a great help in dermatology. The author mostly uses only two levels of magnification: a low power (x40 magnification) for identifying parasites and assessing hairs, and a high power (×1,000 magnification) for identifying bacteria and yeast.

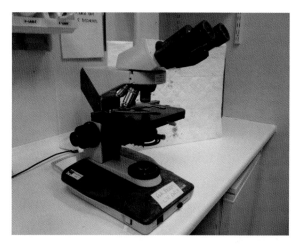

A good-quality and familiar microscope is an important tool in dermatology. Parasites, bacteria and yeasts can all be readily identified in-house, with little expense.

Looking at things under a microscope reveals a world on another scale. It is extraordinary, when you take your eyes away from the microscope, to realize how many yeasts, bacteria, pollen grains, skin scales, plant fibres, etc., are sitting on just one windowsill beyond our normal awareness.

Microscope work can give fast and low-cost information to help our understanding of a skin condition. Sending the samples away to a laboratory gives a time delay and is more expensive, but may be preferable if we do not have the skills and experience to interpret what we see. A good way to gain this experience is to take lots of sample material, to keep and look at part of it ourselves under the microscope, and to compare our findings with the laboratory report when it comes. Microscope work is a visual skill of recognizing normal from abnormal, and correctly interpreting the significance of abnormal. Practice and curiosity will increase skills in this fascinating and useful area.

Plucked Hairs

The technique for collecting hairs is to hold a small clump firmly with the fingers, or with artery forceps, and to pull them out in the direction of growth. The hairs are laid out in parallel, onto a drop of liquid paraffin, on a clean glass slide and covered with a glass cover slip. Taking the time to have the hairs lying in parallel helps with systematic examination. It allows the comparison of adjacent hair bulbs, shafts and tips across the sample. Looking at hairs under the microscope is called trichography.

The hair bulbs, or roots, will either be in an actively growing (anagen) phase or in a resting (telogen) phase when they are pulled out of the hair follicle. Actively growing hair bulbs have a fat, smooth, rounded contour. They often contain pigment and appear bent just before the end. This bend is not present when the hair is in the horse, but occurs as an artefact when the firmly attached growing hair is forcibly pulled out. Resting hair bulbs have a roughened surface contour and are more pointed. They are usually straight and do not contain pigment. The normal adult horse has a mixture of growing and resting hairs. The ratio depends largely on the phase of the moult cycle and how the horse is kept.

It is helpful to look at plucked hairs around areas of hair loss. Broken hair shafts may suggest rubbing or biting of that area, that the horse is itchy, and that the hair loss is self-inflicted. This investigation is obviously not relevant for areas that have been clipped, or where there has been very vigorous grooming. It is useful when horses spend a lot of time unobserved and when itchy behaviour has not been witnessed.

Ringworm can be diagnosed by looking at plucked hairs, but a fungal culture will still be needed to understand which type of ringworm is present. Hairs are plucked with artery forceps, or gloved fingers, from the edge of hairless areas and in the most recently affected parts of the skin. By choosing these parts we aim to pluck growing hairs with an active fungal infection. Once on the glass slide, the adjacent hair shafts are compared across the slide. Normal hair shafts can be thought of as sound logs. They have smooth linear sides and are unbroken. The cortex and the medulla are clearly visible. Infected hairs can be thought of as rotten logs. They are thicker than the normal hairs, and have a fuzzy appearance, with an ill-defined outline. Infected hairs may be broken or bent. The cortex and the medulla are not clearly visible.

A quick and efficient way of picking up fungal elements from the coat is to use a MacKenzie brush technique. Small areas can be brushed

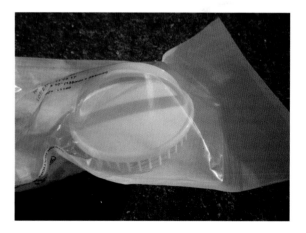

A human scalp brush, which has been sterilized in an autoclave, used in the diagnosis of ringworm. The sterile brush can be run through a large area of hair coat to pick up fungal spores. It is sent to the laboratory for fungal culture, where its size fits neatly onto a Petri dish of fungal culture medium.

with a new toothbrush, fresh from its original packet. The brush is then sent for fungal culture. Large areas are sampled with a sterile human scalp brush. The 7.5cm (3in) wide Denman brush has robust, non-traumatic plastic bristles and a practical handle. It fits neatly into a Petri dish when sent to the laboratory.

A Wood's lamp has a bulb which emits ultraviolet light of a specific wavelength. It can be shone onto suspected cases of ringworm. Hairs which are infected with the dermatophyte *Microsporum equinum*, or *Microsporum canis*, may fluoresce with a bright apple green colour. When fluorescence occurs, those bright green hairs are the ones to collect for fungal culture. If there is no fluorescence, ringworm cannot be excluded, as the horse may have an infection with *Trichophyton* species, or with a non-fluorescing strain of *Microsporum*. *Trichophyton* infections are more common than *Microsporum* infections in the horse. A Wood's lamp is a moderately delicate instrument to have in the back of the car, and the test needs a dark environment and a nearby electrical socket. For these reasons a Wood's lamp is not routinely used on individual cases.

Skin Cells

Cells can be collected from the skin in a variety of ways.

Fine Needle Aspiration

Fine needle aspiration is a good way to get some cells out of a firm skin mass. The aim is to harvest representative material from the mass, which allows us to understand what the mass is. The skin over the lump is carefully cleaned and disinfected. A 21 or 23 gauge needle is pushed into the mass, and a 2ml or 5ml syringe is attached to the needle. The plunger is gently withdrawn to apply suction to the contents of the needle. The suction is released and the

needle is redirected into a slightly different part of the mass. This is repeated four or five times. The syringe and needle are taken out of the mass. The syringe is disconnected from the needle, half-filled with air, then reconnected. The contents of the needle and syringe are gently blown out onto a glass slide, and spread out into a thin layer. The easiest place to sample is the centre of a mass, but this may have less active and less representative cells than at the expanding edge, near the normal surrounding skin. Fine needle aspiration can also be used to sample for deep bacterial or fungal infections. The contents of the needle are expelled onto a glass slide to assess the cells, but also onto a swab to send to the laboratory for bacterial or fungal culture.

Acetate Tape Strips

Tape strips can be used to collect surface skin cells, and single-celled organisms such as bacteria and yeasts. A length of robust, clear adhesive tape is pressed firmly onto the skin to pick up the sample. In haired areas the intervening hair can be clipped or parted before sampling. A drop of methylene blue stain can be placed onto a glass slide, and the tape strip laid onto the slide, on top of the stain. After

Taking samples with acetate tape. The tape is lifted off the horse, flattened onto a glass slide, and examined under the microscope.

30 seconds the stain is rinsed away under the tap. The slide is dried with a paper towel and the tape strip is simultaneously flattened down onto the slide. Bacteria and yeasts can be seen with ×1000 magnification. They take up the blue/purple colour of the methylene blue stain. Bacteria can be recognized as belonging to the rod-shaped or coccoid (round-shaped) bacterial families. *Malassezia* dermatitis can be diagnosed using tape strips.

Impression Smears

Impression smears are made by touching a clean glass slide directly onto a moist lesion, such as the underside of a crust or the contents of a pustule. The slide is allowed to dry, and is then stained and examined under the microscope. Impression smears can be used to diagnose rain scald, or to support the diagnosis of pemphigus foliaceus (PF).

Romanovsky-type stains, such as Diff-Quik and Rapi-Diff, are used for staining cytology

Romanovsky-type stains (marketed as Diff-Quik, Rapi-Diff, etc.) are used for staining cytology samples. They give good definition to most skin cells, bacteria and yeasts, allowing them to be identified under the microscope. These stains are quick and simple to use, and fairly inexpensive to buy. Stain precipitate tends to accumulate in the third, purple-coloured, stain and it needs to be changed regularly.

samples. They give good definition to most skin cells, bacteria and yeasts, and allow them to be identified under the microscope. These stains are quick and simple to use, and fairly inexpensive to buy.

Finding Skin Parasites

A hand lens is useful when searching for small parasites, such as harvest mites (*Trombicula*) or chewing lice (*Damalinia*), found on the skin surface. Visible lice can be individually picked off or dislodged into a Petri dish for identification under the microscope. A cat flea comb or a human head louse comb can be used effectively to separate lice and louse eggs from the hair coat.

Skin Scrapes

Scraping the skin can dislodge loose crust and scale, and some of the surface layers of skin. The author mostly uses a wooden tongue depressor or lollipop stick for scraping. This tool is larger to hold than a scalpel blade, and is incapable of causing damage if the horse moves suddenly. It is easy to retrieve if dropped onto bedding or grass, and produces good-quality superficial scrapings. The chosen area of skin is moistened with a little liquid paraffin and scraped several times in the same direction. It may be helpful to scissor clip a small area of hair before scraping.

It is better to take lots of scrapings, and see lots of parasites, than to take one scraping and miss the diagnosis. This technique is useful for finding *Chorioptes* mites, forage mites and red poultry mites. *Chorioptes* mites can move quickly in the oil film and are often found around the edges of the slide. A scalpel blade is preferable for detaching harvest mites from the skin, as they are firmly attached. Ticks should not be scraped from the skin as their mouthparts will almost certainly be left behind.

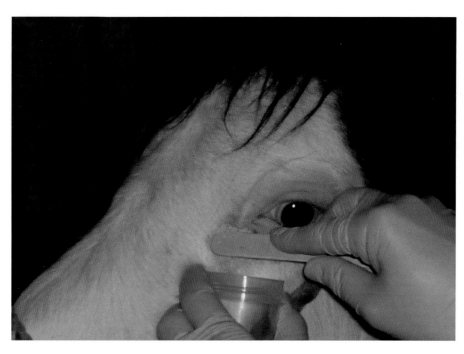

Scraping the skin on a pony's face, using a wooden tongue depressor. The sample collected scale, crust, loose hair and **Chorioptes** *mites.*

BELOW: *The systematic approach needed to examine a slide under the microscope.*

The loose scraped material is transferred to a glass slide, mixed with liquid paraffin, and covered with a cover slip of thin glass to flatten and contain the sample. The slides are examined under the microscope in a methodical way, starting in one corner, to ensure that all of the material is examined.

Deep skin scrapings are rarely needed in horses. *Demodex* mite overpopulation and *Pelodera* dermatitis are both rare conditions in the horse. Deep scrapes are performed with a scalpel blade and continue in the same place until blood starts to ooze from the very small vessels. The mixture of red blood cells and layers of skin are mixed with liquid paraffin on a glass slide and examined.

Acetate Tape Strips

Tape strips can be used to pick up some surface parasites, such as forage mites and pinworm eggs. A strip of good-quality clear adhesive tape is pressed onto the skin surface, peeled off and then flattened onto a glass slide. The length of the tape strip should be chosen to

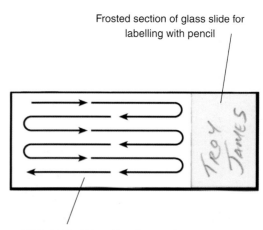

Frosted section of glass slide for labelling with pencil

Lines represent systematic search pattern covering the whole slide

fit neatly onto a glass slide. Samples taken for parasites do not need to be stained, and can be examined using a low-power microscope lens.

Diascopy

An area of red skin can be caused by inflammation, or by bleeding into the skin.

With inflammation there is increased blood flow to the area, and the blood is inside the blood vessels. When bleeding occurs into the skin, the blood escapes from the blood vessels into the surrounding tissue. The resulting red area of skin can look similar in both cases and diascopy helps to tell them apart. A glass slide is pressed firmly onto the skin surface. The colour of the skin under the slide is compared to the colour of the surrounding lesion. If the pressed area goes pale, the red blood is being pushed out of the area. To be able to

A glass slide is being pressed against the red lesion on the skin. There is no loss of redness of the compressed lesion under the slide, compared to the redness of the non-compressed lesion next to the slide. This result tells us that the blood causing the redness has escaped from blood vessels and is in the tissues. The technique is called diascopy. This animal had inflammation of the blood vessels (vasculitis).

move away quickly, the blood must be inside blood vessels, and the lesion is therefore inflammatory. If the pressed area stays red, the blood cannot escape from the pressure and must be outside the blood vessels. The lesion is therefore not inflammatory alone, and may be associated with leaky blood vessels (vasculitis), or with reduced blood clotting ability.

Taking Skin Biopsies

Skin biopsy is a very useful technique. It is often the only way, or the quickest way, to a diagnosis. It is helpful to take biopsies early in the course of the disease, when the active pathological processes can be seen. Biopsy is not a technique of last resort, and early biopsy can save a lot of time and money. Waiting until the lesions have been abraded by an itchy horse, or have a secondary bacterial infection, can allow masking of the primary pathology and frustrate the diagnosis.

Most skin biopsies are taken under standing sedation, with local anaesthetic at the biopsy site. It takes between three and five minutes for the local anaesthetic lignocaine, without adrenalin, to numb an area. The time and expense involved in taking three chunky biopsies, rather than one tiny one, is very small compared to the time and expense of returning for further biopsies if the first sample proves insufficient. Biopsy punches look like little apple corers and come in 2, 4, 6 and 8mm widths. The larger sizes should be used wherever possible, to give the pathologist the best chance of making the diagnosis.

Biopsy material can also be obtained by cutting out a sample with a scalpel blade, or by shaving off a thin slice of skin with a scalpel blade. Shave biopsies do not give full thickness samples but are practical for the coronary bands. A full-thickness biopsy in this area would

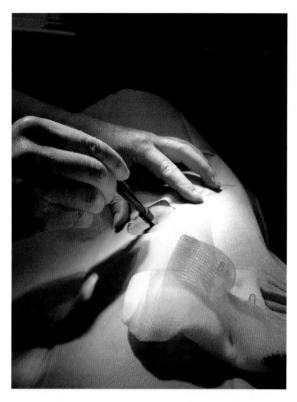

ABOVE: *A biopsy punch is used to take a small core of skin from an affected area. Skin biopsy is generally done without scrubbing and cleansing the skin. It is considered a clean, rather than a sterile, procedure. Excess hair can be cut away with scissors if it is in the way. The area being sampled here already had significant hair loss.*

be likely to cause an undesirable and permanent defect in the hoof wall. Shaved biopsy sites cannot be sutured; instead pressure is applied to stop the bleeding. They are then dressed and bandaged, to promote moist wound healing and to keep the area clean.

Skin biopsies for histopathology are taken *without* close clipping or cleaning of the skin. The overlying hair can be gently cut away from the biopsy site with sharp scissors. The biopsies are taken, the biopsy sites are closed with sutures, and then the area can be cleaned. This approach allows valuable information in the crust, the scale and in the surface levels of skin to be preserved for the pathologist. Gentle handling of the skin sample will give optimal results. Lifting the sample out with a fine needle can be less traumatic than crushing it with a sturdy pair of rat-toothed forceps.

Skin biopsies for histopathology are placed into a solution of 10 per cent formalin. Skin sutures, or staples, can be removed ten to fourteen days after the biopsies are taken. The area may need protection from flies, depending on the time of year. It is important to have up-to-date tetanus protection in place.

In contrast, biopsies for bacterial or fungal culture are taken after close clipping of the skin and a full antiseptic scrub, as for sterile surgery.

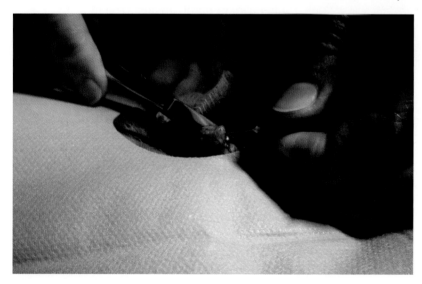

The small core of skin is speared with a needle (right of picture) and gently lifted up. Sharp scissors (left of picture) are used to cut the base of the core free from the body. The core is placed in preservative and sent off for analysis. The small hole in the skin is closed with sutures or staples.

This approach kills off the normal micro-organisms on the skin surface. Any bacterial or fungal growth from the biopsy material will then accurately represent microbes from the deeper tissues, rather than contamination from the skin surface. Skin biopsies for bacterial or fungal culture are rolled in a sterile swab and placed in a sterile container for rapid transport to the laboratory.

It is essential to send the biopsies to a pathologist who is experienced at looking at horse skin. The samples need to be accompanied by a complete and detailed history of the case, by information on where the biopsies were taken from, and preferably by photographs of the lesions. The interpretation of skin biopsies is likely to be thwarted by the presence of secondary bacterial infection, and by the administration of oral or topical steroids. Two weeks of antibiotics just before biopsy, and at least two weeks off oral steroids, are helpful where appropriate.

5 Parasites Affecting the Skin

WHAT IS A PARASITE?

A parasite is an organism that derives benefit for itself from contact with a host (in our context, a horse), but does not give any benefit to the horse in return. Thus the relationship has a cost to the horse and a benefit to the parasite. Parasites may carry pathogens, for example viruses or bacteria, and may leave the horse with a transmitted infection. Parasites can both cause skin conditions and make other skin conditions more complicated. For example, flies visiting an open wound may cause damage by feeding activity and by causing fly-strike. They may also transmit bacteria, which establish a wound infection.

Horses are commonly kept in groups. If several individuals in the group are affected by a skin parasite, such as lice, the parasite may be passing from one horse to another. Alternatively, the affected horses may be picking up the parasite from their shared environment, such as with ticks or harvest mites. When one horse in a group is identified with a parasite, it is helpful to look critically at the other members of the group.

A typical lifecycle of a tick or mite. The eight-legged adult female lays a number of eggs. The eggs hatch to give the six-legged larval stage. The larva moults to become an eight-legged nymph. The nymph moults to become an adult.

TICKS AND MITES

Ticks and mites are members of the class Arachnida, in common with spiders and scorpions. They have specialized mouthparts for feeding on tissue fluids. The mouthparts are on the small front section of the body, and the four pairs of legs are on the larger hind section of the body.

The larva hatches from an egg and resembles a small adult, but has only six legs. The larva moults to become a nymph with eight legs. Nymphs do not have sexual organs and may moult through several stages before emerging as sexually mature adults.

Ticks

Some owners never see ticks on their horses, while for other owners they are a frequent finding. This difference in the number of ticks seen reflects both where in the country the horse lives, and his lifestyle. A stabled horse with little access to pasture, and mostly ridden in a school, will be at very low risk from tick bites. In contrast, a horse at rough pasture, and ridden over moorland, will have a higher risk of tick infestation. The degree of risk will also vary with the time of year and the ambient temperature and humidity. The difference in the number of ticks seen will also reflect whether repellents are used in known problem areas.

The most commonly found tick in the UK is *Ixodes ricinus*, the so-called castor bean, or sheep, tick. Ticks are opportunistic parasites and will mostly latch onto any passing mammal or bird for a blood meal. All ticks need to feed between the changes in their life stages. *Ixodes ricinus* feeds from three hosts during its lifetime. Each blood meal is taken from a different host and the tick drops off into the vegetation between meals.

Ticks are usually found in association with long, dense vegetation, such as bracken or grasses. Vegetation, along with the shade cast by trees and shrubs, or the presence of moderate to high rainfall, ensures that the ticks

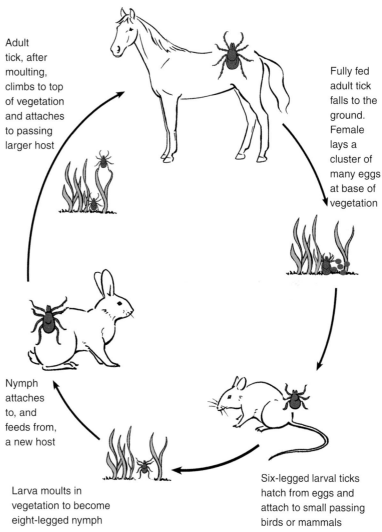

Adult tick, after moulting, climbs to top of vegetation and attaches to passing larger host

Fully fed adult tick falls to the ground. Female lays a cluster of many eggs at base of vegetation

Nymph attaches to, and feeds from, a new host

Larva moults in vegetation to become eight-legged nymph

Six-legged larval ticks hatch from eggs and attach to small passing birds or mammals

The lifecycle of a three-host tick.

do not get dehydrated between meals. *Ixodes* ticks become active when the temperature rises above 7°C (45°F). The larvae find a new host by climbing up a piece of vegetation and waiting. When a mammal or bird is nearby, the tick senses the exhaled carbon dioxide and the vibration, and becomes more active. Holding the vegetation with its hind legs the tick reaches out with its front legs and tries to transfer itself to the passing animal. If the transfer is successful, the tick will then spend some time selecting a suitable place on the skin from which to feed. An *Ixodes* tick needs to feed for several days to get a full meal. It needs to stay on board, even when the host is moving about quickly. Ticks insert their mouthparts deeply into the skin and anchor themselves very firmly. The mouthparts have sets of backward-facing hooks, which create a very firm attachment.

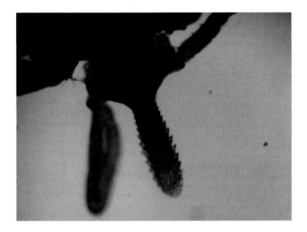

The central mouthparts and two sensory palps of an Ixodes *tick. The photograph is taken through the microscope. Note the row of backward-facing points along the margins of the feeding tube. The mouthparts are deeply embedded in the skin while the tick is feeding. The serrated margins contribute to the security of the tick's attachment to the skin.*

The distensible body of a tick expands gradually as it feeds, and an adult tick can swell to many times its unfed size. Adult ticks tend to feed from larger mammals such as horses, deer, humans and sheep. After an adult female has taken a blood meal she will drop off the host, digest the meal, and may lay a single clutch containing thousands of eggs. The larvae are each approximately 1mm (0.04in) in diameter. They emerge from eggs and will attach to a small host, such as a vole or mouse, for their first meal. After feeding, the six-legged larva drops to the ground and sheds its skin (moults)

to become an eight-legged nymph. Nymphs attach to a new host, feed for several days, drop off, and moult into adult ticks. Unfed adult ticks are about half the size of an adult seven-spot ladybird. After feeding they may expand to become 50 per cent bigger than a ladybird.

Five adult Ixodes *ticks, arranged in a row, to show increasing degrees of abdominal distension. Note that the eight legs, and the structures at the front of the body, are of a similar size across the five ticks. The marked difference in overall size reflects the amount of blood inside the abdomen.*

The prevalent tick in the UK, *Ixodes ricinus*, completes its lifecycle over a period of two to three years. The length of the lifecycle depends on factors such as the length of the winters, and the availability of animals from which to obtain a blood meal.

Removing a Tick

It is important to remove ticks from the skin as soon as they are noticed, and to do this in a safe and effective way. The longer a tick is attached to the skin and feeding, the higher the risk of an infection being transferred to the horse. Squeezing the body of a tick, during a removal attempt, can push the tick's contents back through its mouthparts and into the horse, and may cause an infection to be transferred. Poor removal technique can cause the mouthparts to snap off and be left in the skin, which may lead to an inflammatory reaction, or to an infection.

How do we avoid squeezing the tick or snapping off the mouthparts? A tick remover is quick and simple to use. One user-friendly commercial product is a plastic hook which slides between the tick and the skin, and allows the buried mouthparts to be loosened by twisting. This device puts no pressure on the swollen body of the tick and all of the 'twist and lift' forces are concentrated on detaching the mouthparts.

A plastic tick removal device. These tools are low cost, easily cleaned, and come in different sizes to match the size of the tick. The forked section is passed under the tick, very close to the skin, and the tick is removed with a lift-and-twist action.

Tick removers are available in large and small sizes, to match the size of the tick being removed. They can be cleaned and disinfected after use to reduce the spread of infection. Removal methods such as covering a tick with petroleum jelly or burning it with a cigarette are at best ineffective. At worst they will damage or stress the tick, causing it to regurgitate potentially infected material into the horse.

Tick-Related Problems

Ticks can cause a range of problems for horses. Here are some examples.

Local Reactions to Tick Bites

It is common to have a firm, red, raised area of swelling at the site of feeding. This swollen area may develop a necrotic and ulcerated centre. Some tick bite sites can be very irritating and trigger significant self-trauma. Secondary bacterial infections may develop, which add to the local irritation, and may lead to abscess formation. Swollen and abraded areas attract flies and may result in fly-strike.

Blood Loss

An adult female *Ixodes* tick takes in about 0.5ml (0.02fl oz) of blood during a full and undisturbed feed. This amount of blood is insignificant to a healthy 550kg (1,200lb) horse, but may have serious consequences in foals or in debilitated individuals, which are carrying a high number of ticks.

Disease Transmission

A whole range of tick-borne diseases is found around the world. The UK, as an island nation with a temperate climate, has hitherto been relatively protected. However, the UK may be at increased risk of importing new ticks, and their diseases, owing to the increased number of international animal movements. Climate change has also led to the extension of suitable tick habitat. Relatively mild winter conditions mean that fewer ticks die over the winter months and they can become active earlier in the spring. The tick-borne disease risk in the UK, apart from horses entering from abroad, mainly relates to Lyme disease, which is caused by the bacteria *Borrelia*. The symptoms can be vague and varied, such as running a temperature, lethargy, shifting leg lameness, stiffness or inflammation of the eyes. Horses have a lower risk of being infected than dogs or people. The *Borrelia* infection is transmitted to horses, via the tick, from infected rodents such as mice and voles. Approximately 2 per cent of ticks in the UK are thought to be infected with *Borrelia*. Transmission of *Borrelia* does not happen until at least twenty-four hours after the tick has attached, so regular checking and prompt removal of ticks can protect a horse from disease. Louping ill is a rare tick-borne disease of horses. It is caused by a virus and mostly affects sheep and grouse, but can occasionally cause disease in people and horses.

*An **Ixodes** tick feeding on a person. Ticks are relatively easy to see on people. They are much harder to see, at this early stage of attachment, on the large surface area of haired skin of a horse. Note the characteristic 'head down, bottom up' posture adopted when feeding, with the mouthparts buried in the skin and drawing blood. There is some redness of the skin at the feeding site.*

Management Options

- Check the skin surface for ticks daily, from April to September, in at-risk areas. Remove ticks promptly when they are found, using a safe and effective technique.
- Repellent products containing permethrin, cypermethrin or fipronil may be useful. These products will also kill ticks once they have attached. None is 100 per cent effective, so regular skin checks for ticks are still important.

- Reduce attachment. Smear the lower legs with petroleum jelly before exercise in areas known to have an active tick population.
- Pasture management to reduce the number of favourable tick habitats.

Mites

Chorioptes (Chorioptes bovis/equi)

Chorioptes mites affect sheep, cattle and horses. They are the same mite (*Chorioptes bovis*) in all infested species, but they are sometimes referred to as *Chorioptes equi* when found on horses. Mites are about 0.3mm (0.01in) in length, and feed on surface skin debris. The lifecycle of the mite takes approximately three weeks to complete. The degree of lesion development, and of itchiness, varies between infested individuals. This variation probably reflects a variable hypersensitivity response to the mites.

What Chorioptic Mange Looks Like

Affected horses are often those with 'feather' and have lesions on the lower legs. The cannon, fetlock and pastern areas are most commonly involved. Lesions are more common on the hind legs than on the forelegs. The face, base of the tail, and upper legs can also be affected. The author has recovered mites from the lower trunk of horses with clinical signs only on their legs. The condition is most obvious in the winter months and in horses kept inside, especially on straw bedding.

Itchiness in response to the mites is shown as foot-stamping, waving an affected leg in the air, and biting or rubbing of the affected areas. The lesions are crusts and scabs with underlying wet, raw patches of skin. The patches are typically between 0.5cm (0.2in) and 5cm (2in) in diameter. Some horses may only show excess scale between the bulbs of the heels. Others may carry the mites on their skin and have no

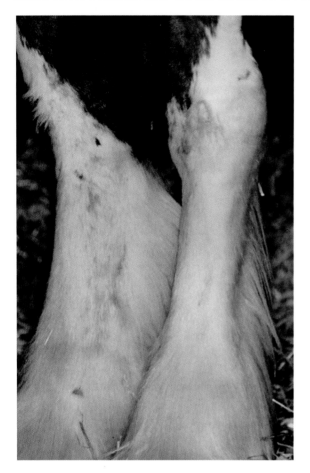

A four-year-old Shire gelding with **Chorioptes** *mites. There are crusty areas all the way up the hind legs. The crusts measure between 0.5 and 5cm (0.2 and 2in) in diameter. This horse has been stamping his feet and rubbing one leg against another, with increasing regularity, for two months. Four other horses on the yard were showing similar signs.*

lesions. Severe cases can be complicated by a secondary bacterial infection of the open lesions.

Making the Diagnosis

Mites can be found in surface skin scale and crusts. Scraping the skin surface dislodges scale and crusts for examination under the microscope. The author feels safer with a wooden lollipop stick or tongue depressor, rather than a scalpel blade, when scraping the lower legs of an itchy horse. The loose material needs to be collected into a container with a tight lid, as *Chorioptes* mites are small and active.

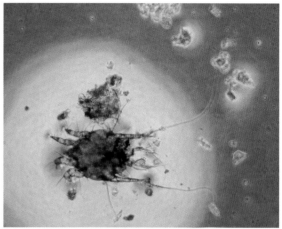

A male **Chorioptes** *mite. The photograph was taken through the microscope.* **Chorioptes** *have legs that stick out beyond the body, a feature typical of surface-living mites. They have cup-shaped suckers on the ends of their legs.*

Treatment Options

The *Chorioptes* mite can survive for more than two months in the environment, away from the horse, especially in cold and damp conditions. It is important to treat both the environment and the horse to prevent treated horses from becoming re-infected from the surroundings. None of the listed treatments can be expected to kill all of the mites and a combination approach is often needed. Treating only the horse and not the environment usually gives a temporary dip in mite numbers, which rapidly recover.

- Remove all of the bedding, clean the stables thoroughly, and treat the floor and walls of the building with a suitable product to kill mites. Allow the area to dry out completely. The grooming kit and tack, rugs and bandages should also be thoroughly cleaned, treated and dried.

- Wash the lesional areas of skin to gently remove crust and excess scale, and to physically reduce mite numbers. Dispose of the washing water carefully as it is likely to contain a large number of mites, which can survive for a period off the horse. Selenium sulphide shampoo is a helpful washing agent, but can sometimes temporarily discolour white hair. Thorough washing and disease monitoring is a lot easier after clipping, but most owners prefer not to clip feathered legs.
- Ivermectin paste, two doses given two weeks apart.
- Doramectin injection, two doses given two weeks apart.
- Fipronil spray, applied until the affected skin areas are damp, four times at weekly intervals, with prior clipping, with or without prior shampooing.
- Lime sulphur shampoo.
- Flumethrin solution, used as a spray or wash.

- Moxidectin gel, two doses given three weeks apart, has been shown to be ineffective.

Some cat or dog flea collars can be helpful to reduce re-infestation, but note that the content of cat and dog flea collars is very variable and this is not a licensed treatment. Some dog flea collars contain amitraz, which is toxic to horses. Always check the active ingredients of the collar carefully with your vet. A single collar is fitted around the pastern. It is very important that the collar has a special section that can break easily if caught up, and a length adjuster that does not allow it to tighten further once it is in place. Some collars will cause a contact reaction with the skin, especially skin that has recently been clipped and washed. One collar should be trialled, and kept under careful observation, on one leg first.

Management Options

- Screen and isolate all horses coming into a yard, or treat on entry.
- Check all of the horses that are in contact with an affected horse, as some may carry

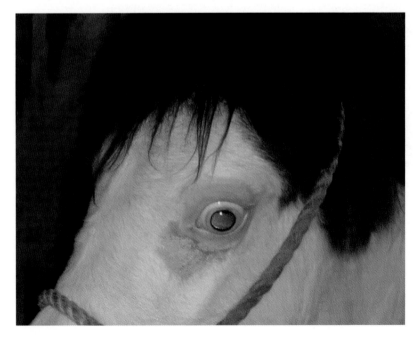

This pony has crusting and hair loss around the eye, and no other visible lesions. Skin scrapes showed **Chorioptes** *mites. Other ponies in the same group had similar lesions on the face, and also on the lower legs.*

the *Chorioptes* mite while showing no obvious signs.

Harvest Mites (Trombicula autumnalis)

The adult and nymph stages of the harvest mite do not feed on animals. They live freely in grassland vegetation. Only the six-legged larval stage of the harvest mite is parasitic. Unfed larvae are dark red/orange in colour and about 0.2mm (0.008in) in length. The larvae are about twice that length after feeding, and paler in colour. Harvest mite larvae only feed on the horse for a few days, so they may only be found intermittently on the skin. In the UK, harvest mites have actively feeding larvae from mid-June to the time of the first frost. They have a patchy regional distribution and tend to be more common on chalk grassland. In affected areas of the country, harvest mites will feed from a wide variety of hosts. The author has found them on sheep, dogs, people, cats, and chickens, as well as on horses. The larvae attach very firmly to the skin and are difficult to dislodge.

Harvest mites are picked up while grazing, or exercising on grass, and are mostly found on the lower limbs and muzzle. Some horses show no response to the presence of feeding larvae, while others display intense irritation. This variation may reflect an itchy allergic reaction in those horses that are sensitized to the mites. Hypersensitive animals tend to show increased irritation and clinical signs earlier in the season, as each year of exposure passes. They may only have low mite numbers on the skin, but a marked degree of irritation.

Making the Diagnosis

High numbers of harvest mites are readily seen as groups of orange mites on the skin of the lower legs and face. Low numbers of mites are usually found tucked away in protected areas, such as between the bulbs of the heel and in the furrow between the two lower jawbones. Careful searching is often required, especially in the hypersensitive horse that might have only low mite numbers present. The mites may only be present intermittently, so searching on different days may be necessary to make the diagnosis.

Despite their bright orange colour, the mites are small and easily missed. They can

A cluster of bright orange harvest mites next to a dog's eye. Only the six-legged larval stage is parasitic. These mites, which are feeding, are firmly attached to the skin. (Photo: C. Kafarnik)

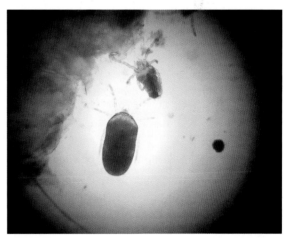

Harvest mite (Trombicula). This photograph was taken through the microscope. Note the orange/red body colour and the six legs of the parasitic larval stage.

be dislodged from the skin with a scalpel blade and often need firm scraping to break their robust attachment. The author generally prefers a wooden spatula for skin scraping, but finds a scalpel blade better for harvest mites. Examination under the microscope shows a red/orange mite with a hairy body and six long legs.

Treatment Options

- Fipronil spray or lime sulphur shampoo, applied directly to the affected areas of skin and re-applied frequently. Neither product is recommended for broken skin.

Management Options

- Move hypersensitive horses to non-affected areas of grazing.
- Horses that graze affected pastures and are irritated by the mites can benefit from greasing of the lower limbs to reduce mite attachment. A non-toxic and non-irritating greasy product will provide a physical barrier. The skin of the fetlock, and below the fetlock, is often affected.
- Cat flea collars on the pastern – see important safety warnings in the section on management of *Chorioptes*.
- Known, repeatedly affected, pastures may be reserved for winter and spring grazing, and used for a hay crop in the summer.

Forage Mites

There are many different types of free-living mite that can be found in hay and straw. They are normally present at low numbers and go unnoticed. Under certain conditions of raised temperature and humidity the mite populations can increase rapidly. This typically occurs with storage of damp hay and straw, in poorly ventilated areas, when the environmental temperature is warm.

What Forage Mite Dermatitis Looks Like

Horses show redness, mild swelling and exudation on areas of skin in contact with the infested hay or straw. Further lesions can occur as a result of rubbing and abrading of the irritated skin. A horse that has lain down on affected bedding may only have affected skin on one side of the body. Horses feeding on infested hay in high nets may have skin lesions over much of the head. Many of the horses sharing the same batch of forage are likely to be affected, as this is an irritant condition caused by unusually high numbers of mites.

Making the Diagnosis

Mites can be picked up using clear acetate tape, and identified under the microscope. High numbers of the same mite species are recovered from areas of affected skin, and from the hay or straw with which the horse is in contact. It is important to distinguish forage mites from mange mites found on the horse, and not to over-interpret the presence of normal numbers of mites routinely found in forage. Affected skin is hot, red and inflamed. A red spotty rash, with or without crusts, can also occur. The associated degree of itchiness is very variable, ranging from mild to severe.

Treatment Options

- Remove all of the affected forage, and sweep and wash out buildings.
- Wash down affected skin to remove mites and any crusted exudate.
- Apply local anti-itch spray or cream to affected skin for a day or two to relieve irritation.

Forage mites are not able to maintain themselves on the horse so, if the infested hay and straw is thoroughly removed, insecticides are not required.

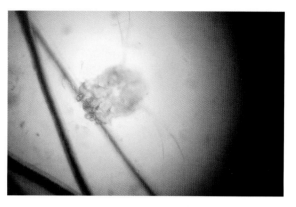

A forage mite (Acarus siro) from the skin of one of the affected ponies. Very high numbers of mites were recovered from the skin and the hay. Note the long hairs, which extend well beyond the body. The photograph is taken through the microscope.

A two-year-old Welsh pony with forage mite dermatitis. This pony was part of a group of twelve sharing the same paddock. The ponies were fed loose hay in a central metal feed rack and in heaps on the pasture. All of the ponies were itchy and showed skin lesions affecting the face and legs. These areas were in direct contact with the hay. The infested batch of hay had recently been bought in. The hair over the lower face has been clipped to show the extensive redness, and bald patches caused by rubbing.

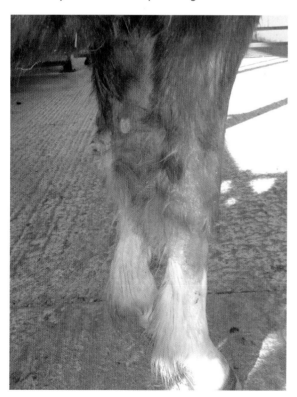

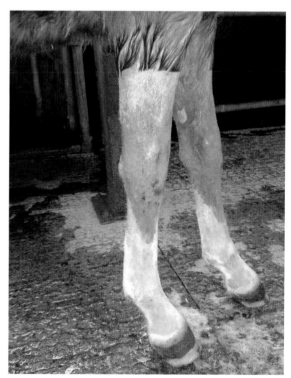

ABOVE: The same pony with affected legs, after clipping. Clipping the hair from the legs is not essential for treatment, but shows the extent and severity of the inflammation.

LEFT: A different Welsh pony from the same group. The photograph shows the forelegs before clipping. There are large areas of hair loss from rubbing.

Management Options

- Buy in good-quality hay and straw.
- Store forage in a dry, well-ventilated area.

Red Poultry Mite (Dermanyssus gallinae)

This is a common parasite of chickens and an intermittent parasite of available mammals, including the horse. Adult mites are about 1mm (0.04in) in length. They change from a grey colour to bright red after a blood meal. The mites live in close association with chickens. They spend the daylight hours hidden in suitable protective places in the structure of the hen house, for example cracks in the wooden walls. The mites lay eggs in the environment, which hatch into non-feeding larvae. The nymph and the adult female stages need a blood meal to continue their lifecycle. They will emerge at night to bite roosting chickens in the hen house. Horses can be bitten if they shelter overnight in places where chickens have roosted, or if chickens regularly spend time in the stables. It is thought that horses do not catch mites directly from chickens. Live mites have been found on chickens in daylight hours, so chickens could transfer mites from the hen house to the stable environment to set up home. Mites transferred to the stable are likely to bite a horse at night when their preferred hosts are all shut up in the hen house. A freshly hatched mite can be breeding in ten days, in warm weather conditions. Adult mites can survive for over six months without a blood meal.

What Red Poultry Mite Dermatitis Looks Like

Small red eruptions and crusts can be seen where the mites have fed from the skin. Any area of the body can be affected, depending on how the mites are reaching the horse. Horses sheltering under infested roof spaces may have lesions on the back. The head and lower limbs can be affected by mites active at floor level. The condition is itchy, often markedly so, depending on the degree of hypersensitivity of the horse and the number of feeding mites. Horses frequently rub and bite at their affected skin, and cause traumatic skin damage.

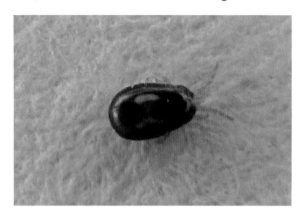

A red poultry mite (Dermanyssus).

Making the Diagnosis

Red poultry mites are mostly active and feeding at night, which means that affected horses are likely to have only low numbers of mites on the skin during daylight hours. The mites can be seen with the naked eye and have a red colour after feeding. They can be collected in coat brushings and identified under the microscope. Samples taken after dark may contain more mites. Any chickens sharing the same environment as the affected horse may also be showing clinical signs. However, normal-looking chickens, with no apparent mites, do not exclude the diagnosis.

Treatment Options for the Environment

All of the life stages of red poultry mites live in the environment, with brief forays by nymphs and adults to feed. Efforts to reduce the mite population should, therefore, be aimed primarily at the environment. Repeated environmental treatments are likely to be required.

- Physical cleaning of the housing is the first step. Take care to remove all of the bedding and droppings before vacuuming out buildings to remove dust, cobwebs, etc. This is followed by scrubbing, hosing and/or pressure washing of the walls, floors and ceilings. Careful use of a blowlamp can also be effective at killing hidden mites.
- Spray the clean environment with permethrin solution.
- Spray the clean environment with lime sulphur solution.
- Dust the clean environment with pyrethrum powder.
- Dust the clean and dry environment with food-grade diatomaceous earth.
- Treat the ends of poultry perches with sticky mite traps, to stop mites from crawling towards roosting birds at night.

DIATOMACEOUS EARTH

Diatomaceous earth is a naturally occurring silicon-rich material composed of fossilized diatoms (tiny shelled algae) from rock sediments. It comes as a fine powder. Freshwater derived, food-grade diatomaceous earth can affect the exoskeleton of red poultry mites. It causes in-contact mites to dehydrate and die.

The extent to which it is possible to reduce the mite population depends on the nature of the environment and the thoroughness of treatment. For example, buildings made of rough sawn timber, with a high surface area of cracks and crevices, may safely harbour a residual population of mites even after rigorous decontamination efforts. The gap between roofing felt and an underlying wooden roof can harbour mites and be a difficult area to treat. Red poultry mites are likely to be encountered for some time after the initial treatment, and after the horse(s) and chickens are moved away from the infested buildings.

Research is under way into red poultry mite control with vaccines, with predatory mites of other species, with fungi which are pathogenic to the mites, and with essential oils.

Treating an Affected Horse

- Short-lived anti-inflammatories are helpful to control the itch, and to reduce the degree of self-trauma to the skin.
- Repellents, for example permethrin, will deter mites from seeking a blood meal, but they require regular and thorough application. Fipronil spray can also be used. These products are unlikely to be totally effective, but they can reduce mite contact in the short term while alternative living space is organized for the horse.
- Separate the horse from affected poultry and, most importantly, from contaminated buildings.

It is also necessary to treat the affected poultry and then move them away from infested buildings. However, do not remove the chickens and leave the horse exposed to infested buildings. In this situation unfed mites will be without their preferred host, and will be more likely to target the horse for a blood meal.

INSECTS

Insects are in a different class from mites and ticks. They typically have a different body structure and a different lifecycle. An insect generally has three clearly distinguishable parts to its body – a head, a thorax and an abdomen. The word 'insect' means 'cut into', evoking the narrow parts of the body which link the head to the thorax, and the thorax to the abdomen. The head has the mouthparts, two eyes and two antennae. The six legs, and the wings, arise from the thorax. It is characteristic of an adult insect to have six legs, in contrast to adult mites and ticks, which have eight legs.

An adult female insect lays eggs, usually preferring a damp place. An egg hatches to release a larva, which is soft-bodied and elongated. Each larva moults a few times as it increases in size. During the final moult the larva remains within the shed skin, which hardens around it to form a dry protective case (puparium). The adult insect forms within this case and, with a miracle of reorganization, typically emerges from the hard case with eyes, wings and legs.

ABOVE: A typical larval stage of an insect. Larvae have soft, segmented bodies and move by undulating waves which run the length of the body.

Fly-Worry

Only a fraction of horses are hypersensitive to insect bites, but most will respond actively to the presence of biting flies. Insect bites range from being mildly irritating to acutely painful, depending on the species of insect. Individuals vary in their response to flies from mild irritation to alarm and bolting. It is helpful to try to distinguish horse behaviour associated with the irritation and discomfort of fly-worry, from persistent itchiness, which may have another cause. Horses generally respond to insects by swishing their tails to protect the rump area. This behaviour is more effective when standing head to tail with another horse, as the rump and head area of both individuals are protected for the same amount of effort. Leg stamping, turning to bite, shaking or swinging of the head, rubbing the ears on the forelimbs and shuddering the skin over the trunk, can all be employed to dislodge flies from the skin. Significant ongoing fly-worry can cause restlessness and anxiety, weight loss and distraction from work. Visible changes on the skin include areas of self-inflicted hair loss, excoriation (skin abrasion) and bruising. Some flies, for example the horse-fly (*Tabanus*), will leave a small bleeding wound at the bite site. This wound is associated with local inflammation and pain. A bee will leave the sting and its associated venom sac in and on the skin, while a wasp or hornet will take its sting away with it.

As well as causing irritation and restlessness, flies can transmit bacteria and are thought to have a role in transmitting sarcoids (see Chapter 6). Certain fly types are attracted to wounds and their larvae can cause fly-strike.

LEFT: A hard, shiny protective case (puparium). The case is formed from the shed and retained skin of the final larval moult. The adult insect develops inside.

For both insect bite hypersensitivity and fly-worry it is helpful to be able to identify, and to have an understanding of, the particular insect types that bother the horse. This knowledge can lead to tailored and more effective protection strategies.

Types of Fly Found Around Horses

House Flies (Musca domestica) and Face Flies (Musca autumnalis)

House and face flies are approximately 6mm (0.2in) in length. They have clear wings and four narrow dark stripes, running in a head-to-tail direction, along the thorax. Groups of flies often look uneven in size as males are smaller than females.

These flies breed in areas with decaying organic material, such as manure and compost heaps. The whole lifecycle can take as little as nine days, depending on the temperature. Consequently, many generations can occur in a season. Adult flies live only three or four weeks and do not have biting mouthparts. They feed on liquids and are attracted to moist skin around the eyes, nose and mouth, as well as to wounds.

This well-managed manure heap is frequently emptied and has a solid concrete base.

Stable Flies (Stomoxys calcitrans)

Stable flies are often seen resting in the sunshine, facing upwards on vertical surfaces such as walls and fence posts. They are about 8mm (0.3in) in length, and grey in colour. They are in the same Muscidae family as house and face flies and can look similar to these flies, as they also have four black stripes on the thorax. Distinguishing features are a broader abdomen and a black proboscis, which points forwards from the front of the head.

They breed in similar sites to house and face flies, for example moist, decaying vegetation and dung heaps. The lifecycle is slower but still produces several generations in one year. Stable flies inflict a painful bite, mostly on the underbelly and legs, and feed on blood. Both male and female flies take blood meals from available mammals. Feeding activity peaks in the early morning and late afternoon, with horses and cattle as the preferred targets.

An adult stable fly (Stomoxys). The black, biting mouthparts protrude beyond the head. The thorax is striped and the abdomen has a spotted pattern.

Horse-Flies (Tabanus) and Deer Flies (Chrysops)

Horse-flies are large, 1–2cm (0.4–0.8in) in length, with chunky bodies, clear wings and large, distinctively shaped eyes. They fold their wings back over the body, giving a streamlined appearance, when resting. Deer flies are approximately 1cm (0.4in) in length, have an overall triangular appearance when resting, and have dark wing bands.

Horse-flies and deer flies are both in the Tabinidae family. They are strong fliers, coping with moderate wind speeds, and can be found significant distances away from their breeding sites. The eggs are laid near water and the larval stages develop in water, mud or damp vegetation. There is only one generation of adults per year, with adults most abundant for about a month over high summer. Horse-flies generally occur later in the summer than deer flies. Male and female flies feed on nectar and pollen, but females additionally need blood meals before laying eggs. Their mouthparts make a cut in the skin and they feed quickly from the blood that wells up. Fly saliva flows into the wound and contains agents which inhibit the clotting of the blood. Female flies will feed from horses and deer, but also from cattle and people. They are attracted to movement and dark shapes, and will persistently chase a moving horse. Flies attack the forelegs, hind legs, underbelly, head and neck, and back, in decreasing order of preference. They leave a painful swelling at the bite site, with a central bloody ooze of fluid. They feed most actively during daylight hours on warm and sunny days.

The attraction of flies to dark shapes has been used as an effective lure strategy to trap these large flies. Traps such as the NZI trap (*Nzi* is the Swahili word for fly) use blocks of colour, of a specific shade of dark blue, to attract flies. This attraction can be enhanced by adding a variety of scent baits such as horse or human urine, lactic acid or acetone.

Bot Flies (Gasterophilus)

Bots have a bee-like appearance. Adults are up to 2cm (0.8in) long. They have a hairy and pointed abdomen, with black and orange coloured bands. The adults are only on the wing for a few weeks in the late summer and do not feed. The female flies lay their eggs on individual hairs. Their persistent hovering around the legs or head, while they attempt to lay eggs, can cause significant irritation to the horse. Different *Gasterophilus* species will lay eggs onto hairs under the jaw, around the lips, or on the forelegs. Larvae emerge from the eggs, and develop in the mouth and stomach of the horse. They are passed, in late spring, in the horse's droppings, to pupate in the soil. The adult flies emerge from the pupae in late summer and the cycle continues. Bot fly eggs can be combed away from the hairs with a cat flea comb. Routine worming contributes to control of the internal stages of the lifecycle.

Mosquitoes (Aedes, Culex)

Mosquitoes have long antennae, long straight mouthparts and long, bent legs. They have a hunched appearance to the body, and a distinctive whining sound in flight. Various mosquito species are active during the warm summer months, most notably in humid weather with low wind speeds. They are found near water for breeding. Mosquito larvae and pupae can be found in water troughs, blocked gutters and buckets of stagnant rainwater.

The females need a blood meal before egg-laying, and inflict an irritating bite. The bitten skin can develop extensive urticaria (see Chapter 7) when large numbers of bites occur. Horses may show signs of fly-worry, or rubbing and scratching behaviour.

Black Fly (Simulium)

Black flies are 3–7mm in length, dark coloured with clear wings, and have a hump-backed appearance. They need clean, fast-flowing water for egg-laying, larval and pupal development. Both sexes feed on nectar, while females additionally take blood meals from mammals to promote egg development. The females prefer to feed on sparsely haired regions of the body such as the head, ears, legs and underbelly, and feed most actively at dawn and dusk. Black fly bites are painful and leave a focal swelling with a central blood-tinged crust. Biological control has been used successfully in parts of the world where black flies are a serious problem. The regular application of a greasy skin cream may give some bite protection to the ears.

Midges (Culicoides)

Midges, also known as gnats, are very small biting flies. Adults are less than 2mm (0.08in) in length, hence one of their North American common names 'No-see-ums'. They live near water and trees. They are weak fliers and have a limited flight range from their breeding areas. Male midges feed on nectar, but the females will take a blood meal from nearby horses before laying their eggs. The bites are irritating, despite the small size of the insect, and some horses become hypersensitive to allergens in the midges' saliva. Feeding is most active on humid days without much wind, at dusk, and somewhat less at dawn. In the UK, midges tend to be on the wing between April and October. African horse sickness, a viral disease transmitted by midges, is not currently found in the UK.

Golden Dung Fly (Scathophaga)

Anyone who has spent time poo-picking a paddock is likely to be familiar with the golden dung fly. These common and abundant flies are found around grazing animals, as they are attracted to fresh droppings. In addition to horse droppings, they can also be seen on and around cow pats and sheep droppings.

The male flies have a golden yellow colour, furry front legs and a furry body. They measure up to 11mm (0.4in) in length. The females are greenish-yellow and hairy and are generally smaller in size than the males. The adult flies feed on insects and nectar. They lay their eggs on fresh droppings and the larvae feed on the dung. Dung flies have an important role in breaking down and recycling dung, and in returning nutrients to the soil. They are harmless to horses.

*A golden dung fly (*Scathophaga*) sitting on droppings. Note the golden fur-covered front legs of this male and the overall yellow colour. (Photo: M. Corke)*

Bluebottles (*Calliphora*) and greenbottles (*Lucilia*) are discussed in the section on fly-strike later in this chapter.

Managing Flies

Reduce the availability of fly breeding sites by reviewing the management of manure heaps, compost heaps, standing water and long damp vegetation.

- Guidelines for the construction of home-made fly traps, suitable for horse and deer flies, are available online.

A well-constructed, clean, tidy and well-managed yard keeps fly breeding opportunities to a minimum.

- Review the location of water troughs, mineral licks, etc., within a field. Try to locate them so that horses can use them with the least fly-worry. Consider the relative location of trees, the prevailing wind direction, stagnant water, the manure heap, etc.
- Utilize physical barriers. For example a fly sheet on the horse, mesh over the stable windows.

- Repellents require frequent and thorough application. They contain ingredients such as DEET, permethrin, citronella or benzoyl benzoate.
- Apply persistent insecticides. For example, synthetic pyrethroids.

Fly-Strike

Fly-strike (*myiasis*) occurs when the larval stage of certain fly species feed on the tissues of a host animal. The species responsible in the UK are as follows.

Bluebottles and Greenbottles

Bluebottle flies usually lay their eggs on the carcases of dead animals and birds. They are also attracted to the soiled and wet skin of living animals (such as the matted perineum of a foal with diarrhoea), to older open wounds, and to ulcerated areas such as fibroblastic sarcoids. The larvae, commonly known as maggots, feed on superficial dead and necrotic tissue and can increase the size of existing wounds. The adult bluebottle (*Calliphora*) measures approximately 1cm (0.4in) in length. It is recognized by its iridescent metallic blue body.

The greenbottle (*Lucilia*) has a shiny metallic green thorax and abdomen. It is of a similar

---

PYRETHRIN AND PYRETHROIDS

Pyrethrin is extracted from chrysanthemum oil. It has a rapid knockdown effect on insects and mites. Pyrethrin is rapidly inactivated by ultraviolet light and so is of limited use in most horse parasite situations. The product has a low toxicity for most mammals, but it can be toxic to cats at high doses, and is toxic to fish.

Pyrethroids, for example cypermethrin, permethrin and deltamethrin, are synthetic derivatives of the natural product pyrethrin. These products are toxic to cats and should be stored carefully to avoid accidental exposure. They are more stable than pyrethrins in ultraviolet light and are generally cheaper to purchase.

A bluebottle, in the centre of the picture, showing the metallic blue abdomen and the duller blue/ grey thorax. Adults feed on nectar. To the left is a greenbottle, and on the far left another bluebottle.

Two greenbottle (Lucilia) flies on a dead bird. Note the metallic green thorax and abdomen. The thorax has small numbers of short, black bristles. The wings are clear, the legs black, and the eyes have a reddish-brown colour.

size to the bluebottle. *Lucilia sericata*, the main species of greenbottle found in the UK, is usually active between June and September. The female fly preferentially lays her eggs on living tissue, but can also be attracted to dead carcases.

The long, slender fly eggs are deposited onto the skin and hatch to produce larvae (maggots). The larvae moult twice into larger larval stages. *Lucilia sericata* larvae are able to break through intact skin and to make fresh wounds. The third and final larval stage drops to the ground to complete its development (pupate) inside a brown-coloured protective case. The next generation of adult fly will emerge from the protective case, about two weeks later.

Bluebottle and greenbottle flies will visit a variety of living, dead and necrotic tissues to feed and to lay their eggs. This movement between carcases, wounds and soiled skin can transfer bacteria and contribute to skin infections. Fly-strike is much less common in horses than in pet rabbits and in sheep. This may be connected to the differences in coat type and quantity, particularly around the perineum.

A more aggressive form of fly-strike is found in tropical and sub-tropical parts of the world. In contrast to bluebottle and greenbottle larvae, the larvae of certain fly types only feed on living tissue and are known as screw-worms (*Cochliomyia/Chrysomya*). Screw-worm larvae do not feed on carrion, and can cause extensive deep tissue damage, and even death, in affected animals.

Treatment and Management Options
• Remove all visible larvae with tweezers. They can be flushed from cavities with warm sterile fluid.
• Keep wounds covered and check them regularly.

- Keep the skin clean and dry, especially in horses with weeping wounds, diarrhoea, discharging sinuses, etc.
- See also the previous section on managing flies.

Fly larvae (maggots) on an area of dead skin. The maggots are of different sizes, reflecting the different larval stages.

Lice

Lice have a distinctive appearance. In contrast to the typical insect they have no wings, and the immature life stages look like miniature adult lice. Horses can be affected by two types of louse.

Chewing lice (*Damalinia/Werneckiella/Bovicola equi*) are 1–2mm (0.04–0.08in) in length, and eat skin scale. They are pale-coloured, and have a wide head with chewing mouthparts. They are usually found over the back and on the neck.

Blood-sucking lice (*Haematopinus asini*) are dark brown in colour and have a narrow, pointed head. They are much larger than chewing lice, at 5mm (0.2in) in length. They prefer to feed on the legs, and near the mane or tail.

Both types of louse are more numerous during the months of the winter and early spring, in horses with a winter coat. They are also more numerous on aged, immature or sick animals, and those in poor body condition.

Lice spend their whole lives on the horse and can be passed to other horses. They are readily seen on the underside of rugs, but they will not survive long away from the horse. Horse lice have a strong preference for horses. Lice found on the yard cat or dog should be specifically

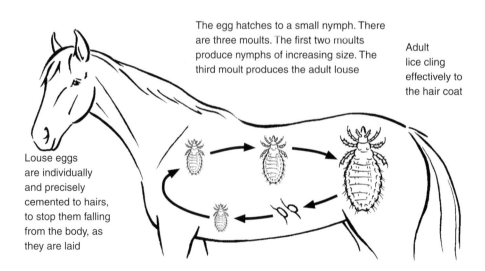

The egg hatches to a small nymph. There are three moults. The first two moults produce nymphs of increasing size. The third moult produces the adult louse

Adult lice cling effectively to the hair coat

Louse eggs are individually and precisely cemented to hairs, to stop them falling from the body, as they are laid

The lifecycle of lice. Lice spend all of their lifecycle on the horse; they do not survive long away from the horse. Different types of louse are specifically adapted to different animals. Horse lice are rarely found on other species, and non-horse lice are rarely found on horses.

The shaggy, unkempt winter coat of a young pony with lice. This pony is in poor body condition, and has recently been transported in close contact with other stressed ponies.

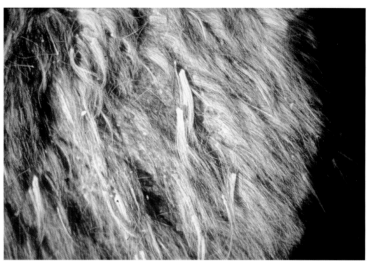

identified, as they are likely to be cat or dog lice, and will not establish persistent infections on the horses.

A female louse cements each of her eggs individually onto a hair shaft. The immature louse emerges from a door (operculum) at one end of the egg. Young lice look similar to the adults and moult to become progressively larger in size.

What Louse Infestation Looks Like

Horses infested with lice tend to have a shaggy, unkempt appearance to their winter coat. Horses often respond to lice by rubbing, scratching and biting the areas of infested skin. The degree of itchy behaviour varies, but can be severe. Patches of hair that are rubbed away leave the horse with a moth-eaten appearance. High numbers of blood-sucking lice can cause anaemia.

Making the Diagnosis

Both types of louse can be seen with the naked eye, but may only be spotted after a careful search. Chewing lice are small and pale, while blood-sucking lice are larger and dark coloured. The white eggs (nits), attached to hair shafts, are often easier to see than the adult lice. The degree of contrast between the colour of the horse's coat and the type of louse present often affects how readily they are seen.

The large hooks on the legs of a sucking louse can be appreciated under the microscope. The size and shape of the hooks are adapted to the diameter of the shaft of a strand of hair. They allow the sucking louse to move around on, and stay attached to, the horse.

Treatment Options

Adult lice are readily killed by many types of licensed anti-parasitic drug. The whole group of in-contact horses should be treated on the same day. The treatments are generally repeated every ten days for three applications, but specific product advice may vary. The itching associated with lice tends to stop a couple of days after effective treatment.

Management Options

Lice are contagious. They are spread by physical horse-to-horse contact, or are transferred on shared brushes, rugs, tack, etc.

- Isolate affected individuals until no further lice or louse eggs are found.
- Keep rugs, tack and grooming kit separate for different horses.
- Treat all of the in-contact horses.

A significant or persistent louse infestation can be a useful indicator of an underweight, stressed or sick animal. It's always helpful to check the well-being and management of an affected horse, as well as treating the lice. Dental disease is a common contributory factor in older horses.

Pinworm (Oxyuris equi)

The pinworm is a gut parasite that can cause irritation around the tail base and perineum of infested horses. The worm eggs are eaten, along with contaminated grass, bedding or hay. They hatch out in the gut. The larvae and adults are mostly found in the colon and cause few clinical signs. Adult female pinworms are 5–8cm (2–3in) in length, and have the sharply pointed tail which gives them their name. They are occasionally seen on a plastic sleeve after rectal examination. Sexually mature females move to the rectum and stretch their pointed tails out of the anus. They lay eggs, along with a sticky substance, onto the skin around the anus. Egg-laying activity, and/or the presence of

*A pony leaning into a tree stump to rub the base of the tail. This behaviour can be provoked by pinworm, but is also associated with insect bite hypersensitivity, sweet itch, **Malassezia** dermatitis in mares, and with lice in the winter.*

eggs, is irritating to the horse. Rubbing at the perineum will dislodge eggs into the environment to complete the lifecycle.

Making the Diagnosis

Pinworm eggs are surrounded by a yellowish, sticky gelatinous material, which gives a pale smeared appearance to the perineal area. The eggs can be collected by pressing clear adhesive tape, sticky side down, onto the skin close to the anus then transferring the tape to a glass slide and examining it under the microscope. The eggs have an oval shape with a flattened opening (operculum) at one end. All of the horses in a group are likely to be infected, so it is helpful to examine several animals.

Tail rubbing provoked by sweet itch, lice or atopic dermatitis can look similar to pinworm irritation, with broken hairs and abraded skin around the tail base. However, horses with pinworm irritation do not rub at other areas of the body.

Treatment Options

- Review recent worming regime.
- Wash the perineum to physically remove the eggs, and to give some relief from itching. Dispose of the washing water away from pasture and forage.

Management Options

- A regular routine worming programme. Pinworm adults and larvae are killed in the gut by most classes of routine wormer, but not all worms may be killed.
- Good stable hygiene.
- Cleaning of areas used as rubbing spots, for example feed troughs and fence posts, as these are likely to be contaminated.
- Feed hay in nets or in raised racks, rather than loose on the floor, as it is less likely to become contaminated by faecal material.

6 Neoplasia Affecting the Skin

Cells in the body normally grow, multiply and stop multiplying in an orderly fashion which is tightly controlled and co-ordinated. In contrast to this, cancer cells grow and multiply, and continue to multiply, in a way which is largely unregulated by the body. They can act independently of the many 'stop' and 'go' signals which regulate a normal cell. Cancer cells are different from the cells they arose from. These differences start with mutations in the genetic code and lead to the different behaviour of cancer cells. It is thought that at least five to seven different mutations are needed to change cell behaviour into a cancerous pattern. If the recipe (the genetic code) is changed, then the outcome of the recipe is different. Some cancer cells are different enough from normal cells to allow the immune system to recognize them as 'foreign', and to attack and dispatch them in an appropriate way. Other cancerous cells are either not recognized as 'foreign', or they manage to evade the detection performed by the ongoing normal immune surveillance.

SOME TERMS EXPLAINED

Neoplasia is the new growth of cells which are not under the control of the body's normal system of regulation. Cells and tumours that behave in this way are termed neoplastic. A neoplasia can be benign or malignant.

A **tumour** is, strictly speaking, a swelling of any kind. A swelling may have many causes, for example local inflammation following the impact of a kick. The term tumour is, however, widely understood to mean a neoplastic growth and is commonly used only with this meaning in general conversation.

The term **cancer** is used to describe any type of malignant neoplasia.

FACTORS THAT MAY INFLUENCE THE DEVELOPMENT OF NEOPLASIA

Genetic Factors

If alteration (mutation) of genes is needed to produce a cancerous cell we can see that cancer is a genetic disease. These altered genes are sometimes passed on to descendants, and sometimes not. Descendants that receive altered genes are predisposed to developing cancer. Between 5 and 10 per cent of cancers in people are inherited. There is not currently a figure available for horses. In grey horses it is recognized that melanoma is associated with the greying gene, but not all horses with the greying gene develop melanoma. It is also recognized that some bloodlines are susceptible to the development of sarcoids, and that some are resistant. However, both melanoma and sarcoids can also occur in horses with no previous history of such tumours in their ancestry.

Environmental Factors

The damaging effects of too much ultraviolet light, and of exposure to tobacco products, or to asbestos are associated with well-documented cancerous changes in people. The unfavourable environmental exposure leads to enhanced rates of gene mutation. Ultraviolet radiation is likely to have an impact on poorly protected horse's skin and to be a factor in the development of squamous cell carcinoma. The thin, sparsely haired skin of non-pigmented eyelids is a common site for squamous cell carcinoma to develop. This is, however, not the whole story as squamous cell carcinoma also occurs on the penis and vulval lips, both body sites that are protected from high ultraviolet impact.

The development of cancer is most likely a result of a complex interplay between both genetic and environmental factors for each individual animal.

DEVELOPMENT OF TUMOURS

Any normal tissue type can transform into a tumour. Skin tumours contain neoplastic versions of the cell type from which they have arisen, for example a melanoma contains neoplastic melanocytes. Skin tumours also

---

BENIGN vs MALIGNANT

Benign tumours can distort the architecture of normal tissue but they will not usually cause the horse to die. They tend to show the following characteristics:

- Limited local invasion.
- No spread around the body (metastasis).
- Individual cells look like the normal cells they arose from.
- Slow growth rate.
- No, or little, necrosis.
- Few dividing cells within the tumour.
- A well-defined edge adjacent to the normal tissue.

Malignant tumours are more destructive of tissues and, if left untreated, will often eventually cause the horse to die. They tend to show the following characteristics:

- Extensive local invasion.
- Spread around the body (metastasis), via the bloodstream or lymphatic vessels.
- Individual cells resemble early precursors of normal cells, or have wide variations in cell size and shape.
- Rapid growth rate.
- Variable amount of necrosis; this can be extensive.
- Many dividing cells within the tumour.
- A poorly defined edge invading the adjacent normal tissue.

contain a structural framework of connective tissue, and a blood supply. Rapidly dividing cancerous cells in a malignant tumour need a lot of nutrients and oxygen from the blood. Parts of a tumour may die because they outgrow their blood supply and may become, for example, the necrotic central cavity in a large spherical mass. The ability to stimulate and organize a new blood supply (angiogenesis) is an important factor in cancer development.

How Tumours are Named

In theory, tumours are named in an orderly way. Benign tumours end with -oma, for example a benign fatty tumour, from fat cells or lipocytes, is a lipoma (these are rare in the horse). Malignant tumours are called carcinomas or sarcomas, depending on which tissues they arise from. Carcinomas come from epithelial tissue, for example a squamous cell carcinoma. Sarcomas come from deeper mesenchymal tissue, for example a lymphosarcoma. This logical naming scheme is not always adhered to. A malignant melanoma is an understandable concept but, strictly speaking, a contradiction of terms.

SARCOIDS

Sarcoids are a type of cancer, arising from the fibroblast cells in the skin. Normal fibroblasts are part of the structural framework of the skin. Fibroblasts make the structural collagen proteins and are very active in wound healing. Sarcoids are the commonest skin tumour in the horse and they should be suspected when any skin mass appears and is persistent. They are most commonly seen in adult horses between two and six years of age. Sarcoids are rarely life-threatening tumours, but they can cause significant problems. They can be difficult to diagnose and treat, and they will often have a

negative impact on a horse's financial value and insurance status.

Causes of Sarcoids

The cause is not clearly understood. Some horses' bloodlines appear to be susceptible to sarcoids while others, for example the Lippizaner, are resistant. These findings suggest that individual horses, because of their genes, can be more or less susceptible to developing the tumours. A cattle wart virus (bovine papillomavirus type 1 and type 2) is thought to have a role in the disease. Flies, which are feeding on the skin, may transmit the virus. Flies can readily move from a sarcoid to another part of the horse's skin, or to a different horse. They can also move from cattle to horses. Fly behaviour may explain the frequent occurrence of sarcoids around the eyes, groin, sheath, and at uncovered wound sites. These are all places where flies are commonly seen, but there is no good evidence for their role in transmission. The development of sarcoids is more complex than a skin infection with cattle wart virus. Skin trauma seems also to have a role to play.

How Sarcoids Behave

The behaviour of individual sarcoids is notoriously unpredictable. Some will remain static for years, while others will grow rapidly and change into a more aggressive type. The lesions will occasionally go away without treatment, or after being damaged. Much more common is the switch to a more aggressive type of tumour after interference or damage. Such unpredictable behaviour has led to problems with insurance cover for this condition. Sarcoids are capable of local expansion and invasion. Only the uncommon malignant type can spread to a distant body site.

A young Shire gelding with an occult sarcoid on the left face. The area is flat, hairless and darkly pigmented. There is a small nodular sarcoid in the centre of the area. The owner takes care to avoid damage to this area from tack, and from rough grazing or abrasive forage.

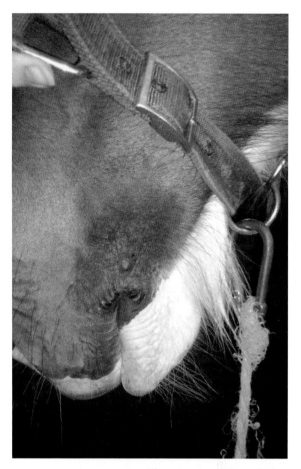

What Sarcoids Look Like

Sarcoids are very variable in appearance and can be confused with many other skin conditions. Many affected horses will have more than one sarcoid and the individual lesions can look very different from one another. Sarcoids commonly occur at thinly skinned areas with little hair covering, such as the groin and inside the elbows. The visual appearance of the various sarcoid types is discussed below.

Types of Sarcoid

There are five main types of sarcoid. It is useful to try to classify individual lesions as the prognosis, and the suitable treatment options, varies between the types.

Occult Sarcoid

These usually appear on the face, inside the elbows, the groin, or around the sheath. They are hairless, approximately circular, and often have an irregular surface when carefully felt. The hair immediately

The same Shire gelding eighteen months later. The affected area has spread up the face. The more recently affected area has the raised and roughened appearance of verrucose sarcoid.

surrounding the bald patch may have a different colour from the rest of the coat. Occult lesions usually remain static, or expand very slowly. They are not painful or itchy and appear not to bother the horse. They have the best prognosis of the various types, but can change to a more aggressive form.

Verrucose Sarcoid

These usually appear in similar sites to the occult type, for example the face, inside the elbows, the groin, or around the sheath. They can also develop at wound sites, especially at any location on the trunk or on the neck. They are hairless and roughly circular in shape. The surface of the verrucose sarcoid has a very rough, warty appearance and a grey colour. They are not itchy or painful. Verrucose lesions usually grow slowly, but can change to a more aggressive form.

Nodular Sarcoid

These are most commonly found around the eyes, the groin, inside the elbows and

sheath. They appear as firm nodules under a layer of skin. When the overlying skin is freely mobile over the nodule it usually has a normal appearance. When the overlying skin is attached to the underlying nodule it can have a scaly, hairless or ulcerated appearance. They are not normally painful or itchy. Ulcerated, or damaged, nodular sarcoids regularly change into a more aggressive form.

Fibroblastic Sarcoid

These can develop anywhere on the body at the site of healing wounds, or historical wounds. They are seen most commonly on the legs. They can develop from less aggressive types of sarcoid which have been damaged. They can also arise spontaneously, especially around the eyes, groin and lower legs. Fibroblastic sarcoids have a red, fleshy, rounded appearance. The surface often weeps or bleeds and is covered with dried scabs and adherent material, for example bedding and dust. The ulcerated surface is attractive to flies and vulnerable to bacterial infection. Despite their raw appearance they are not usually painful or itchy. They may

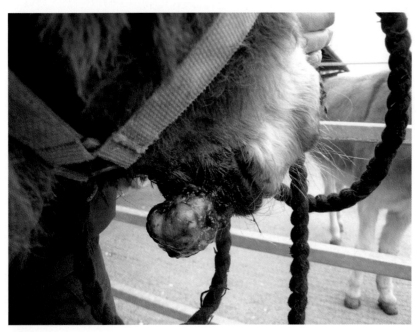

This donkey has a fibroblastic sarcoid on the lower lip, with a typical fleshy appearance. A sarcoid in this location is easily traumatized. (Photo: A. Thiemann)

have a broad base, or hang from a narrower stem of tissue.

Malignant Sarcoid

This most aggressive form of sarcoid is, fortunately, the least common. They have a nodular and/or fibroblastic appearance and may expand rapidly. The lesions are connected to each other underneath the skin, rather than being a collection of separate nodules or ulcerated areas, and can spread along lymph vessels. They can occur anywhere on the body associated with a wound site, or with a damaged sarcoid of another type. Spontaneous development can be seen on the elbows, face or inner thighs.

Mixed Sarcoid

Sarcoids will commonly have different types present in one lesional area. A dominant type is usually evident, for example verrucose sarcoids frequently have an occult border. Sarcoids are classified as mixed when no one type is dominant. They can contain any combination of the five types described above.

Making the Diagnosis

This is a significant challenge. On the one hand it is important to have a definite diagnosis so that rational management, and a prognosis, can be given. On the other hand we know that damaging a sarcoid carries the risk of it changing into a more aggressive form. The damage to a sarcoid may be accidental, or it may be the intentional surgical damage of attempted removal, or of taking a biopsy. A biopsy needs to extract a diagnostic sample from an often complex situation. For example, a wound site may contain a mosaic of granulation tissue, fibroblastic sarcoid and infected tissue. Full thickness biopsies usually give better

information than superficial shave biopsies, and more than one biopsy may be required from the same lesion site. Sarcoids, like granulation tissue, do not contain nerve endings, so local anaesthetic is not required for biopsy. Avoiding the injection of local anaesthetic, not scrubbing the lesion, and not attempting to close the biopsy sites all reduce the physical trauma of the procedure and may reduce the likelihood of subsequent change into a more aggressive form. Since sarcoids take many different forms and can easily be confused with other skin conditions, ruling out other possibilities can help to make the diagnosis. For example, multiple small occult sarcoids can resemble ringworm and a fungal culture can help to exclude this possibility.

Sarcoids can appear at wound sites: they may appear in healing wounds and contribute to early wound breakdown. Alternatively, they can appear at the healed sites of historical wounds, months or even years after the initial trauma. It is helpful to monitor wound sites. Exuberant granulation tissue, exuberant scar tissue, an infected granuloma and a sarcoid can be difficult to distinguish without biopsy. Some wounds may contain a mixture of these components. Wounds should be covered where possible to reduce the risk of fly contact.

Treatment Options

Each individual sarcoid should be assessed and given a veterinary treatment plan, including a plan B in case the first treatment is unsuccessful or provocative. Horses with multiple sarcoids may need different treatments for different lesions, depending on their type and location. Careful assessment and thought are required before starting any form of treatment. The best treatment for some sarcoids may be a combination approach, for example surgical removal followed by medical treatment of any early points of regrowth. It is not possible to generalize on the best approach: each individual sarcoid needs its own risk versus benefit analysis, and a thoughtful treatment plan.

An unsuccessful treatment may provoke a more aggressive sarcoid regrowth. It is important to plan the initial treatment attempt carefully and to aim for a first-time cure. Sarcoids should be treated with respect and 'just trying something on them' can have very unhappy consequences.

Monitoring Only

Some sarcoids, for example occult ones, may form and then remain static for years. If they are not causing a problem, and are at a body site where they will not be abraded by tack, there is the option to actively monitor the situation. Photographs and recorded measurements are helpful aids to monitoring. Care should be taken not to traumatize the lesions, for example with routine clipping, bathing, or grooming. Excellent fly control is recommended for horses with untreated sarcoids.

Medical Treatment

The treatment of small early lesions is likely to have a better long-term success rate than the treatment of large, complex lesions. It is tempting to leave small lesions to 'see what happens'. However, the chances of a definite cure are much better when lesions are diagnosed and treated at an early stage.

Injections into the Sarcoid

Immunotherapy injections into the sarcoid. BCG (bacille Calmette-Guerin) is used to vaccinate people against tuberculosis. It is made from mycobacteria, a type of bacteria, and is a special preparation of this bacteria. The mycobacteria are alive, but their ability to cause

harm is attenuated. This treatment is thought to impact on the sarcoid by promoting the local immune response. BCG can be injected into solid sarcoids, for example nodular and some fibroblastic types. It is not suitable for the flat verrucose or occult types. Injections are given one, two and then three weeks

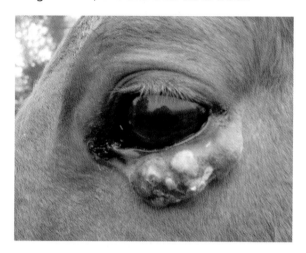

This polo pony has a nodular sarcoid affecting the lower eyelid. There are multiple coalescing nodules with a hard texture. Two BCG injections have been given into the nodules. There is some diffuse swelling around the nodules, which came after the injections. (Photo: A. Schwabe)

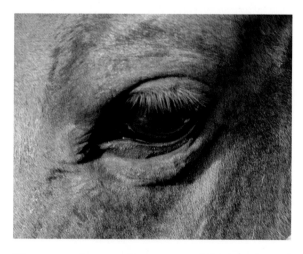

The same polo pony after a course of five injections of BCG into the sarcoid. The photograph was taken four months after the last injection. There has been a good response to treatment. (Photo: A. Schwabe)

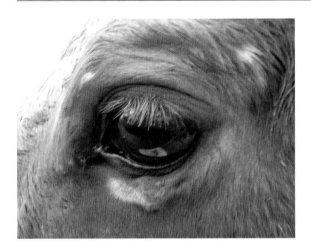

The same polo pony four years later. The nodular sarcoid is just starting to recur, in the centre, just below the lower eyelid.

An oncology nurse preparing cytotoxic medication. The nurse is wearing protective clothing and goggles. Her arms are inside sleeves which extend into the fume cupboard. The sleeves seal around her wrists. Any fumes from the cytotoxic drugs in the cupboard are sucked away from her.

apart. The response is variable, and up to nine injections may be needed. This treatment has moderate to good results for sarcoids around the eye.

BCG injections into normal skin, or frequently repeated injections, can result in a severe allergic reaction. Anti-inflammatory drugs are routinely given, along with the injections, to counter this. Injections are usually given with the horse well sedated, and standing, to allow accurate injection placement and to avoid accidental damage to the eye. BCG is not currently licensed for veterinary use in the UK.

Chemotherapy injections into the sarcoid.
Chemotherapy drugs, such as the cytotoxic drug cisplatin, have been injected directly into sarcoids. This approach gives a high local dose to the sarcoid, reduces the risk of general side-effects, and uses only a small dose of expensive drug when compared to treating the whole horse. The high local dose of drug is very destructive to cells in a non-discriminatory way, and can potentially damage important tissues next to the sarcoid, such as nerves or blood vessels. There is a delicate balance between

killing all of the sarcoid cells to avoid tumour recurrence, and not killing the surrounding normal tissue.

Chemotherapy drugs are potentially dangerous, have restricted availability and need very careful handling within a closely monitored legal framework. They are normally only available through specialist centres. The treated area can become swollen after treatment, and be uncomfortable. Horses are often given anti-inflammatory and pain-killing drugs to help with these short-term adverse effects.

Creams Applied to the Sarcoid
It is important to wear gloves when handling any of these cream products.

5-fluorouracil cream. This anti-cancer drug kills cells, when they grow, by affecting their DNA. It is applied directly to the sarcoid as a cream. The skin can appear hot, red, swollen and painful after application. This treatment should only be applied by a vet.

AW4-LUDES cream. This cream, which was developed at and is regulated by the University of Liverpool, is a mixture of 5-fluorouracil, heavy metals and natural oils. It is applied in different strengths, following a protocol of application times. There can be significant swelling, redness and discomfort of the treated site before an improvement occurs. This treatment should only be applied by a vet, in consultation with Liverpool University. The cream has been used to treat thousands of horses with sarcoids and can produce good effects, with an acceptable cosmetic outcome.

The donkey pictured previously with a fibroblastic sarcoid, one year later. The fibroblastic sarcoid was treated with AW4-LUDES cream. (Photo: A. Thiemann)

Imiquimod is a drug with antiviral and anti-tumour action. It comes as a cream, is applied several times each week, and requires a relatively long course of treatment. There can be hair loss, marked inflammation and loss of pigmentation in the treated area. The treatment is usually stopped until the inflammation resolves, and then restarted.

Acyclovir and ciclofovir are antiviral drugs, which are available as creams. They have been used, by daily topical application, to treat low-grade sarcoids, or as an additional therapy following surgical removal. Their use is logical if bovine papilloma virus is involved in the development of the lesion.

Radiation Therapy

This is the most effective treatment for sarcoids. It has 90 to 100 per cent response rates, compared to up to 70 per cent response rates for other treatment approaches. Radiation therapy is considered the gold standard treatment. However, it requires special facilities, has limited availability and some forms of radiation are expensive.

Brachytherapy

This is a particular type of radiation used for sarcoids. 'Brachy' means short and refers to the short distance that the radiation is able to travel from its source. A brachytherapy radioactive source will release a lot of radiation close to itself, but the dose of radiation drops off sharply away from the source. When the radioactive source is placed inside the sarcoid, the tumour mass will receive a lot of radiation but the surrounding normal tissue will not. Treatment is achieved by placing fine hollow tubing through the sarcoid and placing the radioactive source inside this tubing for fixed lengths of time, and at certain intervals. The success of treatment, with minimal damage to the surrounding tissues, depends on careful planning and calculations of the radiation dose required. Radiation is normally given in a number of small doses, or fractions, rather than one large dose. This fractionated approach reduces the likelihood of adverse effects. Radiation is potentially dangerous for the veterinary staff administering it. Machines have been developed that place the radioactive source into the tubing within the sarcoid, in a standing sedated horse, without the veterinary staff being exposed to radiation. The cosmetic and functional results following radiation therapy are usually good. Preserving the size and shape of the skin is especially important for functional areas such as the eyelids. There is often permanent local hair loss, and loss of pigment in the affected skin and the surrounding hair, after radiation treatment.

Brachytherapy can also be delivered from a **strontium-90** source. This is a good option for sarcoid lesions with little depth. A limited number of specialist centres have a strontium-90 wand. The radioactive strontium-90 gives out beta radiation, which is only capable of penetrating the first 2mm (0.08in) of tissue. The radioactive source is held in direct contact with the affected skin for a calculated timespan lasting only minutes. The wand has a Perspex shield near the active end, and a long handle to allow the person holding the handle to be protected from the source.

Compared to other forms of radiation treatment strontium radiotherapy is very inexpensive to perform, and can be administered to a standing sedated horse. There is a very low risk of damage to surrounding tissues, as the tissue penetration is low. The success of treatment depends on the thickness of the sarcoid, careful planning and calculations of the radiation dose required. With strontium radiotherapy sometimes one dose is all that is required. Because of the limited depth penetration of the beta radiation, strontium can also be used as a treatment to follow surgical removal of the bulk of a tumour.

Teletherapy

This is another type of radiation used to treat sarcoids. 'Tele' means far and refers to the radiation beam coming from a distant source to treat the sarcoid. Suitable radiation beams can be generated by a linear accelerator, a large and expensive machine available at some cancer treatment centres. Teletherapy has been used successfully to treat lower limb sarcoids. Horses need a series of general anaesthetics to receive appropriate fractions of teletherapy and this adds to the cost of treatment.

Surgical Treatment

Whatever surgical method is used it is essential to attempt to remove all of the sarcoid. Any remaining sarcoid tissue will lead to a recurrence of the same type, or of a more aggressive type, of sarcoid. Early wound breakdown after surgery can be a warning sign of persistent sarcoid tissue in the wound. Recurrence rates after surgery alone are generally very high and a plan needs to be in place to deal with new lesions if/ when they appear. Surgery alone is unlikely to be helpful. Surgery is often used to remove as much as possible of the sarcoid before applying another treatment type to the remaining tissue.

It is always difficult to know where the edge of the sarcoid lies, so a wide margin of apparently normal tissue is taken around the sarcoid whenever the local anatomy allows. It is possible to move sarcoid cells through the tissue on the surgical instruments, or to leave some cells behind. Traditional scalpel surgery can be followed up with freezing (cryotherapy), heating (hyperthermia), radiation (brachytherapy) or cytotoxic cream application to the wound bed, to try to kill any tumour cells that remain.

The possibility of moving cells during surgery, or leaving some behind, can be reduced by using a laser to do the cutting, rather than a scalpel blade. With laser surgery, a surgical laser cuts through skin and simultaneously seals off small blood and lymph vessels. Nerves are also cut and sealed. The potential advantages of using a laser for sarcoid surgery are reduced bleeding and less swelling and pain afterwards. Only the light beam is in contact with the skin, so the risk of transferring tumour cells around the surgical site on a scalpel blade is removed. Potential disadvantages of laser surgery are delayed healing and wound breakdown.

After sarcoid removal, wounds may be left open to granulate. This reduces the trauma to the local tissue, and reduces the risk of spreading tumour cells into adjacent healthy tissue when sewing up the wound. The open wound needs to be protected from fly-worry, and kept clean.

WHAT IS A LASER?

The word laser stands for light amplification by stimulated emission of radiation. Most veterinary surgical lasers use carbon dioxide gas as a source of light. Energy is applied to the gas and stimulates the emission of infrared light. The infrared light beam focuses a lot of energy into a small area. The high energy applied to skin cells causes a very rapid heating of their water content, the water turns to steam and the cells are vaporized.

Ligation

This method works by applying firm, even pressure in a ring around a finger of tissue. The blood supply in the tissue is thus closed off. Ligation can be suitable for small nodular, or fibroblastic, sarcoids which have a well-defined neck of non-cancerous tissue between the body and the sarcoid. The special strong, thick rubber bands used for the castrating and tail shortening of lambs can be effective. The bands are applied with a special device, which stretches them open. However, the device will only open a certain amount and this limits the size of sarcoid that can be ligated. This system is not traumatic to the skin and provides sustained pressure.

The use of unsuitably thin or hard ligation material may cause trauma to the skin. The presence of such a cut or wound may provoke the sarcoid to change into a more aggressive form. Other unsuitable ligation material may have insufficient elasticity and only cause partial occlusion of the blood vessels. There will, consequently, be only a partial slough of dead tissue and this can also provoke sarcoid transformation. Ligation can be painful for the horse and deserves suitable pain control.

The sarcoid tissue that is removed at the time of surgery should be sent to a histopathologist. The histopathology report allows us to be confident about the diagnosis and to tailor any further treatment. Looking at the edges of the tissue chunk tells us if we have removed all of the tumour tissue and have so-called 'clean margins'.

SQUAMOUS CELL CARCINOMA

Squamous cell carcinoma is the second most common skin tumour of the horse. It contains neoplastic cells from the epidermis. They are thought to develop in response to the damaging action of ultraviolet light, in areas of skin without protective pigment or a protective hair covering. This explains the most common location being in the non-pigmented, thinly haired, skin around the eyes. The third eyelid, or the white of the eye (sclera), may also be involved. This type of skin tumour is generally seen in older horses, and is equally common in males and females. The pattern of skin pigmentation on the face is an important risk factor for squamous cell carcinoma.

Ultraviolet light is composed of a spectrum of different wavelengths. Ultraviolet B (UVB),

This one-year-old Welsh pony has an extensive area of white hair and unpigmented skin on the face. However, the sparsely haired and thin skin of the eyelid margins is pigmented on both eyes. Much of the skin of the nostrils, and of the lip margins, is also pigmented. This pigmentation pattern gives useful protection against ultraviolet light in areas where the skin is most vulnerable.

with a wavelength of 280–320nm, is thought to be the type of ultraviolet light most associated with skin cancer.

Other common sites for squamous cell carcinoma are on the penis and in the clitoral region of mares, sites that are obviously protected from excessive ultraviolet light. Equine papillomavirus Type 2 has been identified within squamous cell carcinoma of the penis, but has not been proven as a cause of the tumour. Smegma, the lubricating material that allows the penis to slide easily in and out of the sheath, has been thought to be carcinogenic, but this is also unproven.

What Squamous Cell Carcinoma Looks Like

Early lesions look like a small, usually solitary, nodule in the skin. The overlying skin soon erodes away. A raw, fleshy surface is a feature of this tumour, often with a smelly secondary bacterial infection. Squamous cell carcinoma can have the appearance of a shallow crater, an ulcer or a non-healing wound. Alternatively, it may look like a fleshy broad-based mass with an irregular surface. The lesions generally grow and invade local tissues at a slow rate, and are slow to spread from the original site.

An intermittent bloody discharge from the sheath, seen as red spotting on the bedding or on the yard, may be the first sign of problems with a penile lesion. Squamous cell carcinoma of the penis or prepuce is generally faster growing, and quicker to spread, than squamous cell carcinoma at other body sites.

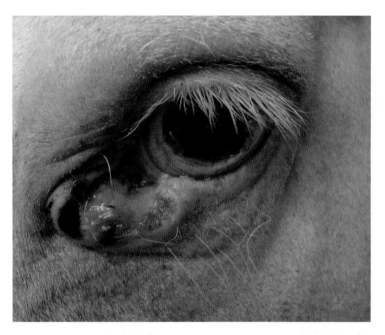

A ten-year-old cob gelding, with squamous cell carcinoma affecting the lower eyelid of the left eye. Note the ulcerated and destructive appearance of the tumour, and the lack of skin pigment in the eyelids. This tumour was treated with iridium-192 radiation therapy. Tubes were placed inside the tumour and the iridium wires were put into the tubes for defined periods to give an appropriate dose of radiation to the surrounding tumour tissue. (Photo: J. Sansom)

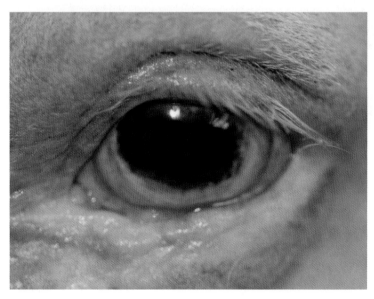

The same cob gelding, showing the left eye two years later. (Photo: J. Sansom)

Treatment Options

The treatment method used will depend on where the tumour is located, how big it is, and the budget for treatment. Squamous cell carcinoma does not usually spread to distant parts of the body, but it can invade the local surrounding tissues.

Tumours on or around the eye should be assessed promptly. There is a risk of losing the eye if the cancer is allowed to grow and invade. Eyelids need to have an accurate size and shape, and a degree of flexibility, to protect and lubricate the eyeball. This functional need limits surgical freedom when cutting out an eyelid tumour. Effective reconstruction and a good outcome for the eye are more likely when the tumour is small at the time of the first surgical attempt.

It may be possible to remove tumours on the penis by local surgery. Sometimes the penis needs to be shortened to effectively remove a tumour. The opening of the urethra is then reconstructed so that the horse can urinate freely.

Tumour tissue, after surgical removal, should be sent away for analysis by a histopathologist. The histopathology report allows us to be confident about the type of tumour we are dealing with, and to assess whether it has been completely removed.

Small lesions, which have been noticed at an early stage, may respond to 5-fluorouracil cytotoxic cream. The person applying the cream must wear gloves.

Brachytherapy Radiation

This is a good option for squamous cell carcinoma with little depth. A limited number of specialist centres have a strontium-90 wand. The radioactive strontium-90 gives out beta radiation, which is only capable of penetrating the first 2mm (0.08in) of tissue. The radioactive source is held in direct contact with the affected skin, or eye, for a calculated timespan lasting only minutes. The wand has a Perspex shield near the active end, and a long handle, to allow the person holding the handle to be protected from the source. Compared to other forms of radiation treatment, strontium radiotherapy is very inexpensive to perform, and can be administered to a standing sedated horse. There is a very low risk of damage to surrounding tissues, as the tissue penetration is low. The success of treatment depends on tumour thickness, careful planning and calculations of the radiation dose required. Radiation is normally given in a number of small doses, or fractions, rather than as one large dose. With strontium radiotherapy sometimes one dose is all that is required. Because of the limited depth penetration of the beta radiation, strontium can also be used as a treatment to follow surgical removal of the bulk of the tumour.

MELANOMA

Melanoma is the third most common skin tumour of the horse. It is a tumour of the melanocytes. Normal melanocytes produce the melanin pigments that give colour to the skin, eyes and hair coat. The majority of horses with melanoma have a grey coat, but horses with any coat colour can be affected.

Tumours in non-grey horses may behave in a more malignant way. Melanoma in grey horses has been shown to have a genetic basis and is linked to the greying gene. The greying gene causes horses to change their hair colour progressively over time to grey. Older grey horses, with a white coat, commonly have at least one melanoma somewhere on the body.

Types of Melanoma

Melanoma tumours can appear in three different forms.

A thirteen-year-old grey gelding with multiple melanoma nodules. These nodules are between 0.5 and 2cm (0.2 and 0.8 in) in diameter, with a smooth surface contour. They are visible under the elevated tail, around the anus, and in the perineal area.

Benign Melanoma

This type affects young horses, up to about seven years of age, of any coat colour. There are usually low numbers of tumours on the face, trunk, legs or neck. Foals can be born with them. The nodules are separate from one another, up to 3cm (1.2in) in diameter, and dark grey to black in colour. They are usually benign.

Melanoma

This type of tumour affects older horses, usually over ten years of age. It is commonly seen around the anus, under the dock, around the sheath, and on the lips and head. Swellings can also appear in the parotid region, near the base of the ear. The nodules may be single, but are more commonly found in groups that may merge together with time. The nodules are most often black, but can contain pale areas, or be entirely non-pigmented. Individual tumours usually grow slowly and can become very large and problematical over the years. They may ulcerate and produce a black, greasy material. Most tumours are benign when they first appear.

Local problems are more common than problems with the tumour spreading to distant sites in the body. For example, ulcerated tumours in the dock region are readily

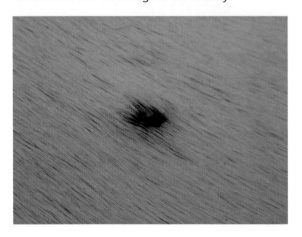

contaminated by faeces and can develop secondary bacterial infections. Masses in this area can prevent the horse from passing faeces in a normal way. Large tumours on the vulval lips, or on the prepuce, may interfere with breeding, with foaling, or with the normal flow of urine.

Malignant Melanoma

This type has the most aggressive behaviour and the poorest prognosis. A proportion of melanomas, over time, will develop aggressive behaviour. They become locally invasive, and spread around the body through the bloodstream, or through the lymphatic system. This tumour behaviour can be seen in older grey horses that have had slowly growing melanomas for many years. Malignant melanoma can also be seen in horses of any age and colour. Tumours in non-grey horses have a tendency to progress more rapidly to local invasion and distant spread.

Making the Diagnosis

Black nodules, appearing in a characteristic site, in a white-haired older grey horse are very typical of melanoma. Tumours in non-grey horses, those in unusual locations on grey horses, and tumours without pigment, may need to be biopsied to confirm the diagnosis. Tumours that are not recognized and treated may spread to distant sites in the body. Horses sometimes develop colic, weight loss or neurological signs depending on where the secondary tumours have grown.

The same grey gelding as in the previous photograph, with a 1cm (0.4in) diameter, darkly pigmented melanoma in the saddle region.

A grey gelding aged twenty-seven, with parotid melanoma. This large mass, between the eye and the ear, has been slowly increasing in size over the past ten years.

Treatment Options

Most melanomas are initially benign; consequently it makes sense to act when they first appear and are small in size. It is tempting to do nothing while they are small and benign, but they are likely to grow into something more difficult to treat.

Surgery

Complete surgical removal is a good option for small separate nodules. It is important to remove all of the tumour tissue with a margin of normal tissue. Remaining islands of tumour cells can sometimes regrow at a rapid rate.

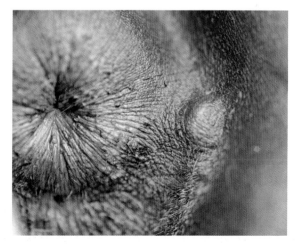

A small melanoma to the right of the anus in a sixteen-year-old grey Irish Draught cross. (Photo: L. Fraser)

Chemotherapy

Chemotherapy drugs, such as the cytotoxic drug cisplatin, can be placed directly into the tumour in the form of beads. This approach gives a high local dose of drug to the tumour and reduces the risk of general side-effects. It uses only a small dose of expensive drug compared to treating the whole horse. The high local dose of drug is very destructive to cells in a non-discriminative way. Cisplatin can potentially damage important tissues next to the tumour, such as nerves or blood vessels. There is a delicate balance between killing all of the melanoma cells to avoid tumour recurrence, and not killing the surrounding normal tissue. Chemotherapy drugs are potentially dangerous and need very careful handling. The treated area can become swollen after treatment, and be uncomfortable. Horses are often given anti-inflammatory and pain-reducing drugs to help with these adverse effects.

Immunotherapy
Anti-Melanoma Vaccine

An anti-melanoma vaccine is available for treating this type of cancer in dogs. Early trials, using the dog anti-melanoma vaccine, have involved small numbers of horses. They have shown tumour shrinkage in most horses receiving the vaccine, but a lot more work is under way to explore any relevance in the horse. The anti-melanoma vaccine is currently only available through specialist centres.

The dog anti-melanoma vaccine contains a section of genetic code (DNA) which codes for human tyrosinase. Tyrosinase is an enzyme, found almost exclusively in melanocytes, which promotes the production of melanin pigments. The dog vaccine, with its bits of human genetic code, can be injected into a horse with melanoma. Human tyrosinase is manufactured, inside the injected horse, from the genetic code information in the vaccine. Human tyrosinase is different enough from horse tyrosinase to be recognized by the immune system. The horse's immune system recognizes it as 'foreign' and mounts an immune response against it. This immune response will be directed against the newly made 'foreign' human tyrosinase, and also towards the horses' own cancerous melanoma cells, which contain tyrosinase.

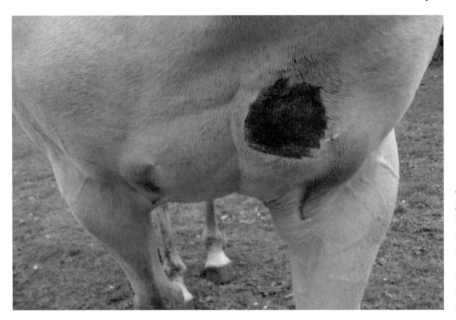

A fourteen-year-old grey mare clipped over a pectoral muscle for administration of the anti-melanoma vaccine. The vaccine had no impact on melanoma size in this horse. (Photo: K. Felton)

Cimetidine

Cimetidine is an antihistamine drug that may also have anti-tumour effects. Its value in treating melanoma is uncertain, and has not been clearly proven in clinical trial work.

LESS COMMON TYPES OF SKIN NEOPLASIA

Skin tumours are, by a significant margin, the commonest type of tumour in the horse. Almost all of them will be one of the three types discussed – sarcoid, squamous cell carcinoma or melanoma. A few of the other, and much less common, tumour types which affect the skin are mentioned below.

Lymphosarcoma

A lymphosarcoma contains neoplastic lymphocytes. Normal lymphocytes are white blood cells which are part of the immune system. Lymphosarcoma involving only the skin (epitheliotropic form) is rare in horses and can mimic a range of other skin diseases. The generalized (multicentric) form is much more common. In this form there can be tumours in the skin, as well as in the lymph nodes, the internal organs and the eye. Horses of any age can be affected.

Mast Cell Tumours

Mast cell tumours are rare in the horse and generally have benign behaviour. They usually occur as solitary nodules on the ears or nose of adult horses of any age. Less commonly they can occur on the trunk, legs or around the eyes. Complete surgical removal of the nodule, or nodules, is usually curative.

7 Skin Diseases Associated with Hypersensitivity

AN INTRODUCTION TO ALLERGIC DISEASE

A healthy immune system provides effective monitoring and surveillance of the body. Immune surveillance is particularly intense at body sites where the inside first encounters the outside, for example the skin, the gut and the lungs. These sites can be thought of as 'gateways' to the body. They are areas where extra immunological 'sentries' are on guard. The immune system discriminates between 'self', which it tolerates, and 'other', to which it responds. The degree of response, or level of sensitivity, to anything recognized as 'other' will vary between individuals. An allergic, or *hypersensitive*, response is a greater than average immune response to an allergen. Animals with an inherited predisposition to developing a hypersensitivity reaction to environmental allergens, including foods, are described as being atopic, or as having atopy. Atopic horses may display their allergy in different ways. Some may have allergic conjunctivitis, with red and runny eyes. Others may have allergic respiratory signs, and others inflammation of the skin (atopic dermatitis). Some horses may have more than one of these allergic conditions at the same time, or throughout their lifetime.

Allergen such as midge saliva in the skin from midge bites, are picked up by the surveillance cells of the immune system. These cells carry the allergen to a nearby lymph node. The cells process and present the allergen to other immune cells. In the majority of horses nothing further will happen. However, in some horses the allergen will be seen as a threat to the body and the immune system will make antibodies against that allergen. The antibodies (immunoglobulin E) sit on carrier cells in the skin. The horse is now sensitized to the allergen.

ALLERGY AND ALLERGENS

Something that causes an allergy – an allergen – is usually a protein of 5 to 100 kDa in molecular weight. A complete allergen can do three things:

1. Sensitize the immune system by causing the production of antibodies against itself, particularly antibodies of the type immunoglobulin E.
2. Meet up with, and bind to, some of those immunoglobulin E antibodies in the body.
3. Cause an allergic reaction as a result of that binding of allergen to immunoglobulin E antibodies.

An incomplete allergen can only cause allergic signs in a previously sensitized horse.

The next time the horse is bitten by midges, the midge salivary allergens bind to the antibodies in the skin and cause the carrier cells to release some of their contents. These contents act rapidly to result in swelling, redness, itchiness and inflammation of the skin. The horse now has an immunological memory of midge salivary allergen and will respond to future midge bites with hypersensitivity.

ITCHY HORSES

Allergic skin disease is often associated with itching. Other common causes of itching are skin parasites and infections. Horses can try to alleviate their itch in a wide variety of ways.

They may rub against solid objects, roll on the ground, scratch with a hind or forelimb, drag the belly along the ground, or bite at their skin. These behaviours may be occasional, or constant, depending on the severity of the itch. The author has seen horses rub to the point of bleeding, and remove very large areas of hair coat by rubbing, and one horse damaged an eye while scrubbing his itchy head against a concrete wall – all to alleviate itching. Long-term itching can cause significant misery and should always be investigated. Itchy horses may be distracted by their itch when working, and severely itchy horses are potentially dangerous to ride or drive.

The itch threshold is a line on an itch scale, above which an individual horse will start to show clinical signs of being itchy. Different horses will have different itch thresholds. Often, a range of factors contribute to itching and their effects add together. Factors such as the ambient temperature, whether anything distracting is happening, and the dryness of the skin, are known to be contributory factors to itchiness in people. It is

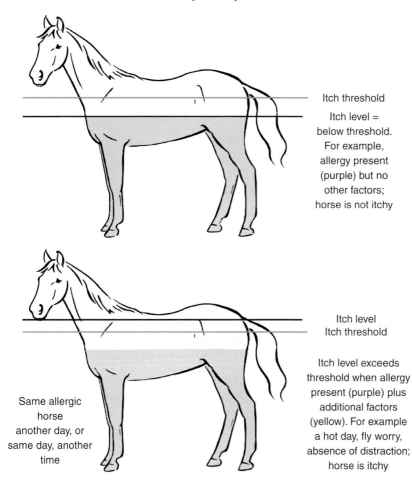

Itch threshold

Itch level = below threshold. For example, allergy present (purple) but no other factors; horse is not itchy

Same allergic horse another day, or same day, another time

Itch level
Itch threshold

Itch level exceeds threshold when allergy present (purple) plus additional factors (yellow). For example a hot day, fly worry, absence of distraction; horse is itchy

The itch threshold. Different factors, which contribute to itching, can add together. The accumulation of factors may make an itchy horse more itchy, or may push a non-itchy horse over his itch threshold.

helpful, in any particular case, to look at all of the possible contributory factors rather than just the obvious. Addressing as many of the factors as possible may bring the horse below his itch threshold without anti-itch medication, or may reduce the amount of anti-itch medication required to drop below that threshold.

The aim of management and treatment is to keep the horse on, or below, his itch threshold. This is achieved by making every management change possible to reduce the horse's exposure to relevant allergens, and to address all of the non-specific contributors to itching. If, after this, the horse is still itchy, then medication is added until the itching is of an acceptably low level and the horse is comfortable. The advantage of tailoring medication so that the horse displays a small amount of itchy behaviour, rather than none at all, is that we know we are not giving unnecessary and excessive amounts of drug.

ATOPIC DERMATITIS

A lot of research has looked into atopic dermatitis in people, experimental mice and dogs. Much less is known about the horse, so some of this explanation is extrapolated from other species, making the assumption that atopic horses are not so very different. Animals with atopic dermatitis have two main differences from non-atopic animals. First, their skin functions as a less effective barrier to the outside world. Poor barrier function allows allergens to penetrate more readily through the skin, and then encounter the immune system. Second, the immune system of atopic animals reacts to allergen in an exaggerated way. This can be an inherited tendency.

What Atopic Dermatitis Looks Like

Horses with atopic dermatitis often show persistent itchiness. The itch may have a seasonal pattern, or occur all year round, depending on which allergens are triggering the condition. Horses can show a range of itch-related behaviour, depending on which part of the body is itchy, and what is available to relieve the itch. They may rub against trees or fence posts, roll on the ground, and bite areas of itchy skin. The desire to scratch in response to itching is a powerful urge. Atopic dermatitis can also manifest as recurrent urticaria (hives), with or without concurrent itching.

Making the Diagnosis

The diagnosis of atopic dermatitis is made based on a compatible history and clinical

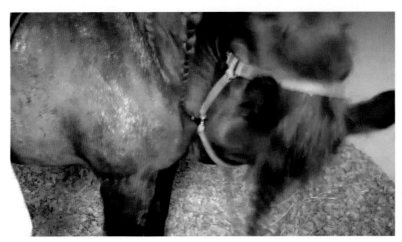

A ten-year-old Fell pony with atopic dermatitis. The gelding was biting repeatedly at his shoulders and trunk.

signs, and by ruling out the many other conditions that may cause horses to be itchy. It is a clinical diagnosis made by the careful exclusion of the other possibilities, and can take a lot of time and effort to achieve. When we have identified an atopic horse we can use either intradermal testing, or blood testing, to identify relevant allergens for that individual. With our current level of understanding and technology the intradermal skin test is the preferred method. These tests will not, unfortunately, differentiate between allergic and non-allergic horses and are not 'a test for allergy'. They can, however, be helpful when we have identified a horse with clinically diagnosed atopic dermatitis. The test results are interpreted in the light of the history, the clinical signs and the management of that horse. To be relevant, the results of the test need to be consistent with the individual horse. The clinical importance of each positive reaction needs to be critically evaluated. If everything fits together the results can be used to avoid the relevant allergens, and to formulate an immunotherapy vaccine.

The reason why intradermal testing and blood testing will not discriminate between allergic and non-allergic horses is because there are too many false positive and false negative results. For example, if a random group of horses were taken and tested, some of them would have positive results on testing, despite having no skin lesions and never being itchy. These are false positives. Some other horses in the group might be itchy and have skin signs and show positive reactions on testing, but could also be false positives as they actually had another itchy skin condition that had not been excluded. Some of the itchy horses might have negative results on testing but clinically, and by exclusion of other conditions, be known to be atopic. Thus negative results do not always mean that a horse does not have atopic dermatitis. We know that horses with atopic dermatitis have, on the whole, more positive reactions than normal horses, but all positive reactions need to be interpreted with caution. Many factors need to be considered when making the diagnosis of atopic dermatitis, and when selecting appropriate treatment.

Management Options

Atopic dermatitis is not curable, but most horses can be given a comfortable quality of life by using a range of management and treatment

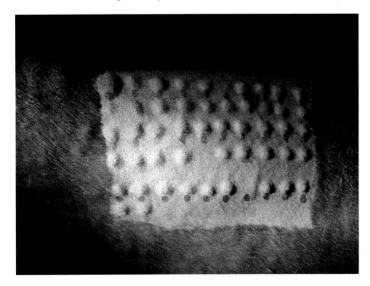

Intradermal testing on the lateral neck of a six-year-old show cob. The area has been clipped. One-twentieth of a millilitre of dilute allergen is injected into the skin, forming a small bump. Each injection site contains a different allergen. Positive reactions are larger red bumps at the site of injection. The results are evaluated thirty minutes, four to six hours, and twenty-four hours after injection of the allergen into the skin.

options. Management is focused on reducing, as much as is possible, the horse's exposure to relevant allergens. It is rarely possible to completely avoid allergen exposure. Practical management options for specific allergens are discussed below.

Storage Mites

Storage mites feed on mouldy bedding and hay, and on imperfectly stored feedstuffs. Bagged feeds are best kept in their original bag with the top closed between feeds. It can be helpful to use a succession of small bags within a reasonable time, rather than have a larger bag of food open for a long period. If stabling of horses is essential then rubber matting can offer a durable and hygienic alternative bedding material. Rubber matting has a much lower surface area than straw, shavings or shredded paper. It can be easily washed down and supports a much lower population of storage mites and mould spores than traditional bedding.

House Dust Mites

House dust mites can occur in rugs and saddle pads. These items can be carefully vacuumed (check that the vacuum cleaner is fitted with a house dust mite filter), washed at 60°C (140°F), thoroughly dried, and sprayed with a product that kills house dust mites. Exposure to direct sunlight can also be helpful. Freezing will kill house dust mites, and will stop them from multiplying, but it will not remove the allergen from the material. House dust mites are ubiquitous creatures and treated items will be readily recolonized after a time. It can be helpful to keep cleaned and treated items in sealed plastic bags until they are needed again, to reduce the rate at which recolonization occurs. House dust mites increase in numbers in warm, humid conditions and are less prevalent in cool, dry environments.

Pollen Grains

Many pollen grains are small, lightweight structures, which can travel long distances on air currents, making them difficult to avoid. Nevertheless, it is worth looking critically at the horse's immediate environment for obvious sources of relevant pollens. Affected horses can be moved away during the limited flowering season of a particular tree or hedge.

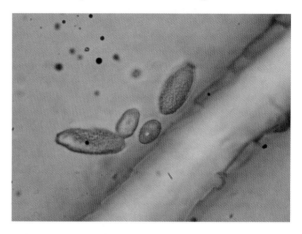

Pollen grains next to a hair shaft. This photograph was taken through a microscope.

Grass pollens are produced by long grasses, in flower, of the type cut for hay. Most horse pasture is so closely cropped that the grass has little chance to flower and to produce pollen. Horses are exposed to grass pollen from nearby areas of long flowering grassland, or from dried flowering grass hay. Horses with hypersensitivity to grass pollens are likely to have less allergen exposure if grazed on short pasture, or fed hydroponic grass or haylage.

Moulds

Moulds grow on damp bedding and produce spores. Horses with hypersensitivity to mould spores are likely to have reduced allergen exposure when turned out at pasture. If they must be stabled, then careful attention should be given to providing a dry, well-ventilated space, with clean, dry bedding. Wet bedding needs to be removed promptly; rubber matting can be a good option. Hay can also be a source of mould spores, and affected horses may do better on haylage.

Insect Control

Insect control is important for all itchy and allergic horses, even if insects are not their main problem. Different causes of itching can add up and push a horse over its itch threshold. See the section on controlling nuisance flies and midges in Chapter 5.

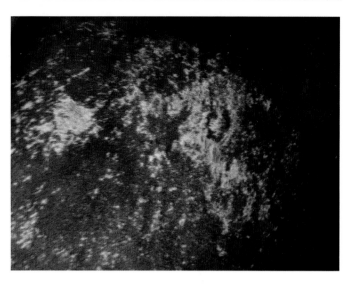

The Fell pony, previously pictured, with atopic dermatitis. The skin over the side of the trunk has hair loss and scarring from past biting behaviour. There is also inflamed, weeping and damaged skin from recent self-trauma.

Treatment Options

Allergen-Specific Immunotherapy (ASIT)

Allergen-specific immunotherapy (ASIT) works by trying to change the root of the allergic response, rather than damping down the end clinical signs. It exposes the horse to slowly increasing doses of the allergens to which he is allergic. ASIT creates a degree of tolerance to the allergens that would previously have triggered an exaggerated reaction. The author recommends ASIT in almost all cases of atopic dermatitis. An immunotherapy vaccine is made up for each individual horse. The contents of the vaccine are based on the results of the intradermal test, serum testing or on both types of test. When selecting allergens for the immunotherapy vaccine, it is important to cross-reference the test results with the horse's history. ASIT is helpful in approximately 65 per cent of cases. Some horses will do well on immunotherapy alone. Others will need medication alongside the immunotherapy, but at relatively low doses. It takes three to seven months, sometimes longer, to see a response

to the vaccine. ASIT is not a quick fix, but is an excellent long-term investment in the health and well-being of an atopic horse.

The immunotherapy solution is injected, usually under the skin of the neck, at gradually increasing time intervals. The volumes and time intervals of the standard schedule can, if required, and in consultation with your vet, be tailored to the response of the individual. If horses have a good response to this treatment the injections can be continued lifelong. The commonest adverse reaction to immunotherapy injections, seen in less than one in five horses, is swelling at the injection site. This swelling goes away, without treatment, after one or two days. Although serious adverse reactions are rare, horses can have an allergic reaction to the injections. Allergic reactions vary in severity from itching and urticaria, to diarrhoea, colic or difficulty breathing. Adverse reactions almost always occur within an hour of injection, and when the doses of immunotherapy are increasing, so keep an eye on your horse during these times. Don't give the injection and then leave your horse unattended. Contact your vet immediately if adverse reactions occur. Fortunately such reactions are rare and are usually seen only in the early stages, as the volume of injected vaccine increases. The first five injections, when starting a course of immunotherapy, are generally given under veterinary supervision as this is the period in which adverse reactions are most likely to occur.

Bathing

Bathing a horse, with a non-irritating shampoo, can physically wash allergens and microbes away from the skin. Shampoos are available with added ingredients and they can be chosen to help the individual horse. Shampoos containing chlorhexidine, or ethyl lactate, can help to control secondary infections. Colloidal oatmeal is useful for dry, itchy skin, and sulphur/salicylic acid can help to remove excess skin scale (dandruff). The choice of appropriate shampoo is likely to change with time, as the skin condition changes, and they are best used thoughtfully rather than habitually. Bathing in

EXAMPLE OF AN ALLERGEN-SPECIFIC IMMUNOTHERAPY SCHEDULE

Day Number	Amount for Injection (in ml)
1	0.2
15	0.4
29	0.6
43	0.8
64	1.0
85	1.0

Then 1.0ml, given every twenty-eight days, thereafter.

The immunotherapy solution contains proteins, which are sensitive to temperature, and needs to be stored in a refrigerator.

cool water, or simply hosing down, can give temporary relief to an itchy horse.

Antihistamines

Antihistamines have a low overall level of efficacy, but can be helpful in some individuals. They tend to work better when given in advance of an allergic challenge, rather than after the event. They are quickly metabolized by the body and need to be given two or three times through the day. A variety of antihistamines have been given to horses. It may be helpful to try a few different types, particularly types from different antihistamine families,

Hosing down can give short-term relief to an itchy horse.

Extensive and severe skin trauma caused by self-excoriation. This horse was severely itchy and rubbed himself at every opportunity, against every available surface.

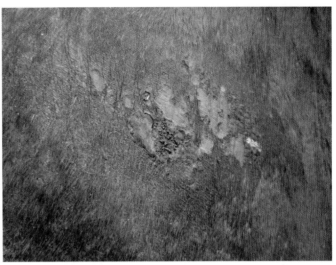

to see if they help an individual horse. A treatment trial of ten or fourteen days is generally long enough to assess any effect. Care should be taken with horses in work as antihistamines can cause variable degrees of sedation. Sedation is usually less apparent after the first few days of treatment. The antihistamine hydroxyzine should not be given to pregnant mares as it can cause damage to the foetus. Clemastine has minimal absorption by mouth in the horse.

Fatty Acid Supplementation

The addition of fatty acid supplementation to the feed has been shown to cause concurrent increases in fatty acid levels in the blood. Unfortunately, there is not a reliable concurrent reduction in the level of itchiness. Fatty acid supplementation in dogs can help antihistamines and corticosteroids to work more effectively, and they are sometimes used for this purpose in horses. Evening primrose oil, fish oil and flaxseed oil have all been used as sources of fatty acids, either alone or in combination.

Steroids

Steroids (glucocorticoids) are generally effective and helpful for atopic dermatitis. The amount given, and the frequency of dosing, needs to be tailored to each individual case. Horses with hypersensitivity to certain pollens may need treatment only for a month or two. The fast onset of action, and the short treatment window, make steroids a logical choice for this limited allergy period. Horses with year-round clinical signs may need an ongoing, low, alternate-day dose to keep them comfortable. Prednisolone tablets, 5 or 25mg, are the most widely used form of steroid in itchy horses. Localized itching can be treated with the local application of a steroid spray or gel. It is sensible to wear gloves when applying steroids to the skin. They will have an effect on human skin, as well as on the horse's.

FOOD HYPERSENSITIVITY

Hypersensitivity to dietary allergens is thought to be rare in the horse and there are very few well-documented cases. This may be a genuine situation, or it may be a result of not looking for the condition. Itchy horses rarely have rigorous food trials performed and we may consequently be missing the diagnosis. Intradermal testing and blood testing for food allergies are not currently accurate or reliable enough to replace the need for a restriction diet trial. Hopefully, this situation will change, with new developments in the future, as diet trials can be challenging to perform to a good standard.

The choice of feed for a diet trial is based on what the horse has eaten before. The idea is to feed a new type of food, for a period of three to six weeks. Choose something that the horse has not eaten before, which will keep him healthy for six weeks. The new diet needs to have completely new content, not just a change of brand with similar ingredients. All supplements and treats should be stopped for the duration of the food trial. At the end of the trial we ask the question 'Is there food sensitivity or not?' and put the horse back on all aspects of the original diet. To make a diagnosis we need the horse to improve on the diet trial, get worse on the original diet, and improve again on returning to the diet trial. If we do not have these three aspects of the diagnosis, the changes could be coincidental. If the horse does improve, gets worse and improves again through the diagnostic process we can go on to ask 'What is he sensitive to?' We can expose the horse to the diet trial diet, plus one other foodstuff for a week at a time, and patiently accumulate a list of individual feedstuffs that can be fed safely. While all this is going on it is helpful to keep the management and environment as unchanging as possible so that food is the only variable.

URTICARIA

Urticaria, or hives, occurs when granule-containing cells (mast cells and basophils) release the contents of their granules in the skin. The chemicals within the granules cause blood vessels to leak their fluid and protein contents into the skin. This process forms localized inflammatory bumps or wheals. The number of wheals varies, from a few to several hundred, and they can cover most of the body. The shape of the wheals is variable. Shapes include rings and 'S' shapes, as well as the most common flattened dome shape. The size of an individual wheal varies from 2mm (0.1in) to 40cm (16in) in diameter. Pushing a finger onto one of the wheals displaces fluid within the underlying tissues and forms a pit, which slowly fills in again with time. A mass filled with a pool of liquid will pit on pressure, but will not retain the shape of the finger. (In contrast to this, a solid mass will not pit on pressure.) The trunk and neck are the areas mostly commonly affected by urticaria, but wheals can appear anywhere on the body. Some wheals leak inflammatory fluid, which dries to form a crust, and some are itchy. The hair over the wheals is generally retained and may stick up as the skin contours change. Urticaria usually appears abruptly and may disappear in a day or two. Some cases recur frequently and others persist for weeks and months.

Urticaria is a common clinical sign in the horse. It has a wide variety of possible underlying causes. Diagnosing the cause in any individual can be time-consuming, and requires a patient and thorough approach. A proportion of cases have 'idiopathic' urticaria,

A horse with extensive urticaria over most of the body. There are both dome-shaped and ring-shaped lesions of various sizes. The horse has no associated itching. (The white spots in the photograph are hailstones!)

POSSIBLE CAUSES OF URTICARIA

Exercise
Physical pressure
Vasculitis
Foods
Transfusion reactions
Infections with, for example, bacteria or ringworm
Stress
Drugs, for example the antibiotic penicillin
Insect stings and bites
Vaccination
Atopic dermatitis
Temperature, being in a cold or hot environment

meaning that we do not understand the causes and mechanisms. As with 'lameness' the term urticaria is not a diagnosis – it is a description of what we can see, with many possible causes resulting in the same clinical sign.

urticaria if the underlying diagnosis is atopic dermatitis.
- The possible adverse effects of drugs need to be balanced against the severity and implications of the urticarial reaction. Horses with urticaria are usually well in themselves, but the condition is visually striking.
- Corticosteroids are usually effective in controlling symptoms.
- Antihistamines, for example hydroxyzine, work proactively and are most helpful if given before the arrival of seasonal or other predictable urticarial episodes. They may also be useful in chronic urticaria.

ANGIO-OEDEMA

Angio-oedema is a more serious and much less common condition than urticaria, although urticaria commonly precedes or accompanies it. The swellings in angio-oedema are large and ooze serum or blood onto the skin surface. The head, lower legs and lower body are most commonly affected. Swelling extending to

Treatment Options

- Avoid, or change, the underlying causes where they are known.
- Allergen-specific immunotherapy can be helpful for recurrent

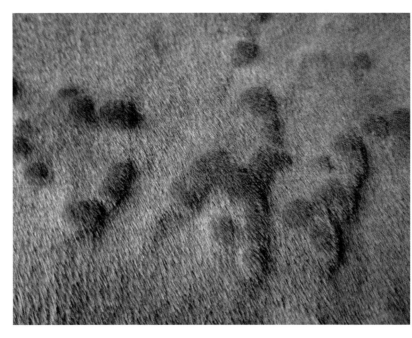

Urticaria is readily noticed on horses that have been clipped. The hair over the swollen skin sticks up and can give the illusion of being a different colour.

the larynx and pharynx requires emergency treatment, as it can block the breathing and be fatal.

SWEET ITCH

Sweet itch is also known by the names insect bite hypersensitivity, *Culicoides* hypersensitivity, or summer recurrent dermatitis. It is caused by an allergic reaction to allergens in the saliva of *Culicoides* species midges (also known as gnats). When the insect takes a blood meal from the skin, salivary allergens are injected into the horse. Midges live near water and trees. They are not strong flyers and have a limited flight range from their breeding areas. Male midges feed on nectar, but the females will take a blood meal from nearby horses before laying their eggs. They feed on humid days without much wind, most actively at dusk, and somewhat less at dawn.

Sweet itch has been described in most horse breeds, and is well recognized in some family lines. It is helpful not to breed from affected individuals. Certain breeds, for example Icelandic, Friesian and Shire horses, are thought to be at increased risk of developing the condition. Iceland is one of the few places in the world – along with New Zealand, the Hawaiian Islands and Antarctica – that does not have a species of *Culicoides*. A case of sweet itch is seen when both the genetic predisposition and the source of allergen are present together in an immunologically susceptible individual.

The seasonal timing of clinical signs coincides with the appearance of biting midges. The timing will change depending on local conditions in a particular year. In the UK, in an average year, midges were traditionally thought to emerge first in April and be active until October. Recent *Culicoides* research has shown that midges can survive for up to three months at 10°C (50°F) in the

laboratory. Adult midges normally survive no longer than twenty days, but this lifespan may be extended by favourable winter conditions. Trapping studies of wild midges in Belgium have shown that small numbers of live adult *Culicoides* can be caught throughout the winter period.

What Sweet Itch Looks Like

The first signs of the condition are, generally, seen in young adult animals. They show an increased extent and severity of signs with the passing of subsequent allergy seasons. Horses show skin signs and itchiness at the places where the midges feed. This may be along the topline, under the body, or both on top and underneath, depending on the species of midge involved. The space underneath and between the lower jawbones may also be affected.

Early signs include small bumps on the skin, which are very sensitive to the touch. Horses will rub on any available surface, may roll frequently, and can drag their bellies along the ground for relief. Vigorous rubbing and scratching damages the skin and causes hairless and traumatized areas. The root of the tail, the

This horse was very itchy. The hairs of the mane are short and broken from being rubbed frequently. The skin on the right of the picture is thickened and the overlying hair has been rubbed away.

The underbelly of a mare with sweet itch. There is thickening and abrasion of the skin, along with crusts and broken hairs.

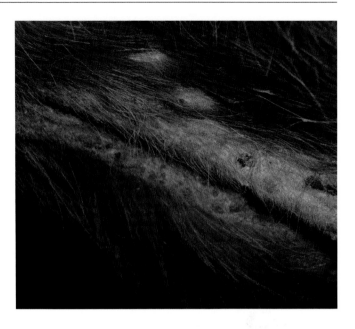

mane and the forelock are commonly rubbed into ragged tufts. Skin bacteria may multiply at the damaged sites and cause a secondary bacterial infection. Persistent itchiness can cause distraction from work, irritability and weight loss. Individuals affected over a number of allergy seasons can have marked thickening and folding of the skin, and a completely rubbed out mane and tail base.

Making the Diagnosis

Sweet itch needs to be differentiated from pinworm or mite infestations, and from allergies to food, other insects and environmental allergens. There is no reliable diagnostic test currently available. Making the diagnosis relies on recognizing the clinical signs and the seasonal pattern, ruling out other possible causes and assessing the response to management and treatment measures. Midges can be seen in the environment, or found feeding on the skin down between the hairs. Sweet itch is not curable, but most horses can be given a comfortable quality of life by using a range of management and treatment options.

Management Options

- Move affected individuals to breezy, free-draining pasture, and away from trees and wet areas.
- Provide a barrier between insects and the skin around the periods of dawn and especially dusk. A variety of fly rugs with hoods, tail guards and belly sections are commercially available. These should be well-ventilated and light enough to avoid sweating on warm days. They also need to be snug-fitting, and robust enough to avoid damage or dislodgement by rubbing and rolling. Some are impregnated with insect repellent; others have sewn-on pockets which can hold insect repellent, which is regularly renewed. Stabling can be midge-proofed with fine mesh screens over windows and half doors. Note that *Culicoides* are very small insects. Mesh screens designed to block mosquitos are generally not fine enough to exclude midges.
- Horses will often learn to stand in the air flow of field or stable fans.
- Remove manure from the premises regularly.
- Repel insects to reduce the frequency of bites. A variety of insect repellents is available. Repellents contain ingredients such as DEET, permethrin, citronella or benzoyl benzoate. Oil and water emulsions, for example Avon Skin-so-Soft bath oil diluted 50:50 with water, can also be helpful.

Repellents need to be applied thoroughly and frequently during the midge season. (A 1 per cent topical deltamethrin solution has been shown not to prevent midges from feeding on experimental horses.)

- Give routine vaccinations, for example against influenza and tetanus, in the winter months.
- Introduce fish to nearby ponds to eat midge larvae.

It is helpful to put rigorous management options in place to reduce, or avoid, the need for medication.

Treatment Options

- Bathing can give short-term relief by cooling the skin and washing away surface crust and scale. Suitable shampoos may include colloidal oatmeal, sulphur and salicylic acid, or chlorhexidine, depending on whether the primary issue is itch, scale or secondary infection.
- Allergen-specific immunotherapy works by giving small and steadily increasing doses of prepared insect extract to the horse. The injections are given over a period of several months before assessing efficacy.

A rug designed to protect from insect bites. Note the separate body rug with tail guard, belly section, neck rug, and head section with ear protection. Various combinations of these sections can be worn, depending on the local insect species present and their preferred feeding sites on the horse. Rugs are available in a range of sizes, as this Shire horse shows. They need to be tailored to fit the individual very well, while being comfortable and not too hot to wear through the summer.

The idea is to induce tolerance, rather than hypersensitivity, in the immune system towards insect allergens. This form of treatment has good future potential for sweet itch but more research is needed to formulate an appropriate and reliable immunotherapy vaccine. Midge saliva is known to contain a range of salivary proteins.

- 'Sweet itch vaccine' is a preparation of a bacterial cell wall which alters the horse's immune system away from an allergic response. The initial product was an injection. Current trials are looking at a capsule, given every week by mouth. There is no peer-reviewed published data yet available on these products.
- Corticosteroids are potent anti-inflammatories that can work quickly to relieve the symptoms. However, they have wide-reaching effects on the body and can precipitate laminitis in susceptible horses. Corticosteroids are available in a variety of formulations including by injection, as tablets, as gel and as a skin spray. Their use needs to be tailored to the individual horse and tapered to the lowest effective dose.
- Antihistamines work best in a preventive role, with medication starting before the beginning of the sweet itch season. Their efficacy is highly variable between individuals and one class of antihistamine may suit one individual better than another. Take care with working animals as antihistamines may cause drowsiness. They are contra-indicated with pregnancy and some medical conditions.
- Nicotinamide, also known as niacinamide, is the water-soluble active form of vitamin B3. It can be used as a supplement in the feed, and/or as a skin gel, to modify the immune response. It is thought to improve the barrier function of the skin, to reduce water loss through the skin and to have anti-inflammatory effects in people. These

effects have not been clearly shown in horses.
- Ice packs, wet towels from the fridge and local anaesthetic cream can give short-term relief from itching.

HYPERSENSITIVITY TO BITES FROM OTHER INSECTS

Other biting insects, apart from *Culicoides* midges, are thought to cause or contribute to allergic skin disease in sensitized horses. The balance and the species of insects responsible for a particular case will depend on the local environment, the geographical location and the immune system of the individual horse. Black fly (*Simulium*), horse-fly (*Tabanus*), stable fly (*Stomoxys*) and mosquito may be involved individually, or in various combinations. There may be enough similarity between salivary allergens from different insect species that a horse sensitized to one insect will have an allergic reaction in response to the bite of another insect type. In contrast to *Culicoides* hypersensitivity (sweet itch), particular horse breeds have not been associated with hypersensitivity to bites by other insects. However, protective measures that effectively repel or block midges will also reduce the number of bites by the larger insects. If the problematical insects can be identified, it is helpful to understand something of their lifecycle and habits, so that relevant control measures can be put in place.

CONTACT ALLERGY

This condition results in inflammation of the skin and may appear as redness, swelling, weeping fluid and variable itching at the affected area. There is usually a history of direct contact with the cause of the problem. An allergic reaction needs a period of sensitization before clinical signs are apparent, so there may have been contact over a lengthy period before a problem occurs. This makes it more difficult to identify the cause, as the same thing will have been tolerated without problems in the past. The clinical signs are similar to a contact irritation, the only difference being that irritation can occur at the first exposure and does not need a period of sensitization. Contact allergy tends to occur in a single allergic individual, when a group of horses are exposed to the same allergen. In contrast, contact irritation is likely to affect the whole group. Contact allergy has been reported, for example, to some insecticidal products, certain plants in the pasture, some shampoos, chrome and certain bedding materials. Inflammation of the skin is only seen in the areas corresponding to direct contact with the problematical material.

Contact allergy can be treated by washing the affected area with lots of water, and a very mild shampoo, in order to dilute and remove any remaining allergen. Marked inflammation, especially if associated with itching and self-trauma, can be treated by the short-term application of corticosteroid cream or spray to the affected area. The cause of the allergy can then be avoided, as much as possible, in the future.

8 Contagious Skin Diseases

A contagious disease is spread by contact between horses. Skin diseases can be spread by direct contact, for example one horse touching another, or by indirect contact, for example two horses rubbing on the same fence post. The incidence of contagious skin disease can generally be reduced by good stable and hand hygiene, and by having separate rugs, grooming kit, bandages, etc., for each horse.

RINGWORM (DERMATOPHYTOSIS)

Ringworm is a fungal disease. The name refers to the common circular appearance of the signs on the skin, and to the old and mistaken belief that it was caused by a worm.

The types of fungus that cause ringworm are called dermatophytes. Those affecting horses are in the family *Trichophyton* or *Microsporum*. These fungi live on keratins, which are the structural proteins of hoof, skin and hair.

Ringworm spores survive for long periods in the environment. They can be transferred from infected animals onto fence posts, fly sheets, dandy brushes, etc. When spores come into contact with damaged skin an infection can develop. The skin damage may only be a slight abrasion, for example a friction rub from tack, but it is enough to disrupt the surface barrier layer of the skin. Flies may also carry ringworm spores between animals and may damage the skin by feeding. Hyphae (elongating tubes) emerge from the ringworm spores and move into the skin protein keratin. Ringworm hyphae produce enzymes that break down keratin. The breakdown products provide them with a source of nutrients and allow them to invade hairs, hair follicles and the surface layers of the skin. The hyphae invade the shafts of actively growing hairs and damage them. This damage can cause the hair shafts to break off and be shed.

Examples of Dermatophytes Affecting the Horse

Trichophyton equinum. The most commonly isolated horse dermatophyte: adapted to horses.
Trichophyton verrucosum. The normal host is cattle.
Trichophyton mentagrophytes. The normal host is rodents.
Microsporum equinum. Adapted to horses.
Microsporum canis. The normal host is cats, despite the name.
Microsporum gypseum. Found in the soil (not adapted to a particular animal).

What Ringworm Looks Like

Ringworm infection typically looks like an expanding circular patch of partial, or complete, hair loss. Individual areas are 0.5–2cm (0.2–0.8in) in diameter. They commonly occur at frictional sites, such as under harness or tack. The number of patches varies from one to dozens. Young animals or debilitated animals often show higher numbers of lesions. Urticaria can be a feature early in the course of the infection. *Trichophyton* infections tend to show more complete hair loss at the affected patches than those caused by *Microsporum*. The exposed skin may appear normal, scaly, crusty or inflamed. The horse may have no apparent itch, a moderate level of itchiness, or anything in between. Signs are visible on the skin between one and three weeks after the initial infection. Ringworm is easily spread between horses.

Making the Diagnosis

Confirmation of the suspected diagnosis of ringworm is important. This is done by growing the fungi on a fungal culture plate. A positive diagnosis rules out other skin conditions. It also justifies the significant amount of work involved in treating the horse, the horse's kit and the environment, and allows the likely source of infection to be identified and addressed.

Hairs can be plucked, with artery forceps or with a gloved hand, from the edge of a circular hairless area. Alternatively, the affected areas can be brushed with a sterile scalp brush to collect fungal elements. Choosing to sample from the most recently affected areas will increase the likelihood of a positive culture. Some strains of *Microsporum equinum* and *Microsporum canis* show a bright green colour under ultraviolet light. A Wood's lamp can be used to highlight the infected hairs. Fluorescent hairs are ideal hairs to pluck and send to the laboratory for fungal culture. Hairs can be examined under the microscope to diagnose ringworm infection, but a sample still needs to be cultured in the laboratory to identify which type of dermatophyte is involved. It is preferable to send fungal samples out to an experienced laboratory, with ideal growth conditions, rather than to use in-house culture media.

Fungi grow slowly in the laboratory, in comparison to the majority of bacteria. A culture is only judged to be negative when

Patches of hair loss and skin scale on the left side of the muzzle. This horse has a ringworm infection. Fungal culture grew **Trichophyton equinum**.

there is no growth after ten to fourteen days. Isolation of the possibly infected horse, and hygiene measures, are often started before the infection is confirmed. Such precautionary measures are unlikely to harm the horse and they may significantly reduce the spread of this highly contagious disease.

Treating Ringworm Cases

Most healthy horses will clear themselves of a ringworm infection, without treatment, over a period of one to four months. When hairs enter the resting phase of the hair growth cycle, the hair is naturally shed and the infection cannot maintain itself. Most horses develop an immune response to the fungi, and maintain this for a short time after infection. The immune response is useful to prevent immediate re-infection from a contaminated environment, or from an infected grazing partner. Horses receiving medication that suppresses the immune system, or horses with PPID/Cushing's disease, may struggle to clear an infection, or may have frequent relapses.

Treatment does not reduce the amount of time that ringworm takes to clear. So why do we treat ringworm cases? The main reason for taking some action with a ringworm case is to reduce the number, and the spread, of the highly infectious fungal spores. This reduction is important both on the horse and in the environment. Reducing the number of spores will reduce the risk of a group of horses becoming infected. It will also reduce repeated infections in the same horse from the long-lived spores in the environment. Treating a case may also reduce the extent of the lesions.

Ringworm is potentially contagious to the people who are in contact with an infected horse. People may become infected directly from the horse, from contaminated rugs and grooming kit, or from the contaminated environment.

Treatment Options for the Horse

- Isolate infected horses away from contact with other horses. It is helpful to do this at the first suspicion of ringworm, as the definite diagnosis may only come weeks later.
- Wear disposable gloves and washable overalls and boots when handling an infected horse. These measures reduce the risk of transferring the infection to another horse or person, or getting infected yourself.
- Long hair can be cut away from around the affected areas with scissors. Contain the cut hair and burn it. Treat the scissors with a fungicidal product.
- Heavily crusted and matted areas can be scraped with a wooden tongue depressor to remove much of the spore-laden hair and skin scale. Contain the scraped material and burn it, along with the tongue depressor.
- Wash the whole horse with a suitable product, for example enilconazole solution, miconazole/chlorhexidine shampoo, natamycin solution, or lime sulphur solution. The bathing interval will depend on the product used, for example a miconazole/chlorhexidine shampoo is used twice a week until the infection has resolved.
- Allow affected horses access to sunshine, where possible.

Treatment Options for the Environment

- Clean the environment thoroughly. Remove all bedding and hay from affected stables and, preferably, burn it. Clean all visible signs of dirt and dust with detergent and water. Spray the clean surfaces with a suitable product, for example household bleach diluted 1:10 with water, or one of the commercial fungicidal disinfectants. Hand-pumped pressurized spray bottles are useful for spraying cleaned surfaces in buildings.

- Horticultural foggers, containing antifungals such as miconazole, can be used to decontaminate enclosed areas after physical cleaning. Fumigation with formaldehyde may also be an option.
- Thoroughly clean tack, grooming kit, rugs, etc., and treat with a suitable product, for example enilconazole or natamycin solution.

Management Options

- Control contact with the likely source of infection, depending on the type of dermatophyte isolated. For example it may be relevant to control rodents with *T.mentagrophytes*, or treat a yard cat infected with *M.canis*.
- Check tack, rugs, harness, grooming kit, stables, fencing, clipper blades, etc., for causes of skin abrasion and skin damage. Remember that ringworm can only take hold when there is a break in the protective skin surface.
- Do not share tack, grooming kit, rugs, etc., with other horses.
- Vaccination, containing a mixture of *Trichophyton* and *Microsporum* strains, is available in some European countries. Vaccination can be used to reduce the risk of infection, or to enhance the immune response when there is an active infection. It may be helpful in persistently contaminated environments, to reduce the severity of repeated infections.

PAPILLOMATOSIS

Equine papilloma virus can cause increased cell numbers (hyperplasia) in the epidermis. The virus causes epidermal cells to divide and multiply, resulting in focal warty growths. Papillomatosis may occur in the following forms.

Foal warts (congenital papillomatosis). The virus can cross the placenta, inside an infected mare, and affect the skin of the developing foal. Foals may be born with a single wart or a small cluster of flat warty growths. Foal lesions are usually seen on the trunk, head or neck. A growth may also be seen on the mare's placenta. Foals are generally not bothered by the lesions, which are not painful or itchy. Unlike grass warts, the foal lesions do not spontaneously resolve and may require surgical removal. The foal does not make protective antibodies to equine papilloma virus and may go on to get grass warts when older.

Grass warts (viral papillomatosis). This condition is mostly seen in young adult horses, when they are encountering the virus for the first time and are grazing together in groups. The virus is passed by direct contact between horses and by contact with infected pasture. A small break in the skin, perhaps caused by repeated minor trauma from grazing, is needed to allow the virus to enter and become established. The skin cells that are infected with the virus multiply very quickly to form warty lesions. Only the surface epidermal layers of the skin are affected and they expand outwards.

Warts are most commonly seen on the muzzle and around the lips. They are small and pale in colour, with a rough surface texture resembling a cauliflower. They generally increase in number over time. The lesions may merge together to form plaques, and may bleed if traumatized.

Papillomas in young horses resolve spontaneously over a period of three to four months, as the horse mounts an effective immune response to the virus. Horses that recover spontaneously are protected against recurrence of the disease.

Older horses are occasionally affected, for example if they have not encountered the virus before, or if their immune system is compromised. The lesions in older horses can be at any site, but most commonly affect the perineum, vulva, groin and penis. They tend to be slow-growing single lesions and are much less likely to resolve spontaneously. Antiviral cream, such as imiquimod, can be helpful if the horse will tolerate frequent application to the affected area. Surgical removal of the papilloma is curative.

AURAL PLAQUES

Aural plaques are a common skin condition in horses. They are likely to be caused by a papilloma virus and transmitted by flies, including black flies (*Simulium*) which feed preferentially on sparsely haired skin. Aural

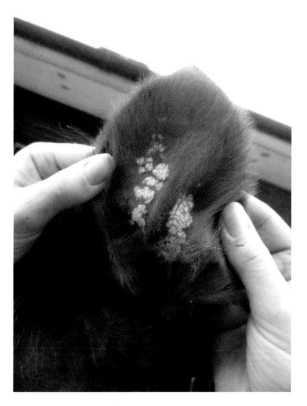

Aural plaques on the inner aspect of the ear of a Thoroughbred gelding. The warty appearance and the white colour are typical of the condition. Both ears were affected. There were no associated problems.

plaques start as very small and shiny de-pigmented areas of skin. They are found on the inner surface of the ears, and first appear in the summer months. At this early stage they are easily missed on horses with grey ears, or those with significant hair at this site. The areas gradually enlarge and thicken to become raised, circular and pale-coloured. The surface texture is rough, or covered in small, closely packed finger-like projections. The amount of associated flaky dandruff varies considerably. Individual plaques may merge together to cover large areas of the concave aspect of the ear. Sometimes only a single ear has aural plaques.

There is a sharp contrast between affected and adjacent normal skin. Most horses show no response to the presence of the plaques. However, some horses show pain or irritation, and will shake their ears and resist ear handling.

Much less common locations are the medial thighs, underbelly and groin, with or without concurrent ear lesions. Horses with plaques in this location are predominantly geldings rather than mares.

This is largely a cosmetic problem with no reliable treatment options. Plaques are unlikely to resolve spontaneously. Given the sensitivity of the ears, treatment is only justified in severely distressed individuals and may result in long-term resentment of ear handling.

BACTERIAL SKIN INFECTIONS

Horse skin is not sterile; it has a normal population of bacteria on its surface, which cause no harm to the horse. However, bacteria increase in number, and may invade below the skin surface, when the local conditions change. For example, the normal surface bacteria may move into an abraded area of skin. The exposed tissue, the moisture and the raised local temperature of the abrasion can support bacterial multiplication and an infection may take hold. Bacterial skin infection is usually secondary to something else happening. It is always worth considering what the underlying causes could be, if they are not obvious. Horses with PPID/Cushing's disease can have persistent and recurrent bacterial infections, as they have an impaired immune response. Only a proportion of bacterial skin infections are contagious.

Bacterial Folliculitis

Bacterial folliculitis occurs when bacteria multiply in the hair follicles and cause inflammation. *Staphylococcus aureus*, *Staphylococcus pseudintermedius* and *Streptococci* species are most frequently involved. The condition is associated with minor trauma to the skin, contact with dirty tack, or having a dirty skin. Bacterial folliculitis can be seen in any location but frequently occurs on the trunk. It can also occur at the back of the pastern as part of the mud fever complex.

What Bacterial Folliculitis Looks Like

The lesions of bacterial folliculitis appear as small tufts of hair, which stand more upright than the adjacent hair coat. Feeling the area reveals a collection of small bumps, each approximately 4mm (0.16in) in diameter. The skin may feel damp with exudate, or crusty

where the exudate has dried. The area can be swollen. The lesions are often painful and horses react when they are touched. As the lesions heal, they become flat and the overlying hair is lost. The multiple small patches of hair loss can give a similar appearance to a ringworm infection, and they occur in similar areas.

Making the Diagnosis

Taking a swab from the affected area allows the bacteria to be grown in the laboratory, and the correct antibiotic can be identified.

Treatment Options

- It is sensible to consider the bacteria as potentially contagious, even before the culture results are back. The bacteria that cause strangles (*Streptococcus equi* var. *equi*) can also cause bacterial folliculitis.
- Clip long hair from around the lesions without causing further skin trauma.
- Wash the affected skin with a chlorhexidine or povodine-iodine solution. Allow a contact time of five to ten minutes, then rinse and dry thoroughly.
- Horses may need sedation and/or pain-relieving drugs to allow effective clipping and cleaning to take place.
- Dressings, where practical, can provide pain relief and allow antibacterial agents, such as silver, to be held against the area. It is important to change dressings regularly and not allow the skin to become over-hydrated.
- Antibiotics may be needed in some cases. Their use should be based on bacterial

An area of inflammation and crusting over the back, exactly corresponding with the contact area between skin and saddle. This gelding was exquisitely sensitive to touch in the affected area. The lesion did not recur after treatment, when the horse was subsequently ridden in a correctly fitting saddle. (Photo: S. Dyson)

culture and sensitivity testing, to understand which bacteria are involved and which antibiotics may be effective.

Management Options

- Isolate affected horses.
- Wear disposable gloves and washable overalls when caring for the affected horse.
- Keep water buckets, grooming kit, headcollars, etc., allocated to only one individual.
- Think about the safe disposal of contaminated washing water, dressings, etc.
- Groom horses regularly to remove loose dirt and debris from the hair coat.
- Keep tack supple and clean.
- Have saddles fitted professionally, and reassessed on a regular basis as the age, the bodyweight and the level of fitness of the horse change.

Resistant Bacteria

When bacterial infections do not respond to logical therapy the possibility of antibiotic-resistant bacterial strains should be considered. Bacteria that are resistant to antibiotics are widely recognized as a potential problem. Your vet can give detailed advice on management.

Rain Scald (*Dermatophilosis*)

Rain scald is a skin infection caused by the bacteria *Dermatophilus congolensis*. These bacteria are widespread in the environment. *Dermatophilus* can only establish a skin infection when both skin damage and skin wetting are present. Wetting of the skin can occur, for example, from prolonged sweating or from persistent rainfall. Dormant bacteria are activated under wet conditions and are able to swim in the moisture on the skin surface. They are attracted to the carbon dioxide released from the skin, and can move into any small breaks in the continuity of the skin surface. Once *Dermatophilus* have passed through the surface barrier layer they can multiply and invade the epithelial layer of the skin. The immune system of a healthy horse will stop the bacteria from invading deeper layers of the skin. Rain scald usually affects a number of horses in a group. Bacteria can be transferred to other horses under wet conditions, when the bacteria are active and mobile on the wet skin surface of the infected horse.

Multiple outer skin layers, along with the bacteria, form thick scabs on the skin. *Dermatophilus* bacteria can remain dormant, and protected within these scabs, for long periods. The scabs are a source of re-infection for the individual horse, and a source of contamination for the environment when they fall off. The dormant stage of *Dermatophilus* can survive for more than a year in the environment.

What Rain Scald Looks Like

The typical scabs are often felt before they are seen. The hair coat is matted together by a hard scab close to the skin surface. Scabs tend to be larger, and to include more hair shafts, when the coat is long. Horses often show discomfort or pain when a scab is picked off. The underside of the scab is often domed and contains a small pocket of pus. The exposed oval of skin, where the scab was, generally has a smooth and pink appearance. White or pink areas of skin are frequently more severely affected than pigmented skin. The scabs are typically found over areas that take direct rainfall, such as the back, the neck on the side where the mane does not lie, and the hips. Scabs, and subsequent hair loss, may form downward-pointing triangles at body sites where water runs through the coat. When the scabs eventually fall off they usually take a tuft of hairs with them.

Lesions may also be seen on the lower legs, which are areas frequently exposed to wetting

The back of a young horse recovering from rain scald. This horse is part of a group of young horses at pasture with no shelter from the rain. They have been repeatedly affected by episodes of rain scald. The picture shows a layer of thick crusts growing out with the hair coat. The distribution of crusts mirrors where the skin and coat are wetted down during episodes of heavy rain.

and minor abrasions. *Dermatophilus* infection on the legs can be a cause of the mud fever complex. Horses with extensive areas of affected skin may be unwell and off their food, but most horses seem undisturbed by the condition. Urticaria can sometimes be seen alongside rain scald.

Making the Diagnosis

Pus, from the underside of a fresh scab, can be swabbed and sent to the laboratory for bacterial culture. Unfortunately *Dermatophilus* are not easy for the laboratory to grow and visual identification of the bacteria can be diagnostic. The fresh pus can be smeared onto a glass slide, stained and examined with a microscope. *Dermatophilus* have a typical appearance under the microscope. The diagnosis can also be made by taking a skin biopsy for histopathology. It is useful not to clip, or to scrub, the skin before biopsy as most of the diagnostic clues are in the surface crust.

Treatment Options

A healthy horse that is moved to a dry and non-abrasive environment will usually recover spontaneously from rain scald over several weeks to months. The treatment options whilst the horse is infected are as follows.

- Isolate affected horses, as rain scald is potentially contagious.
- House affected horses, where possible, to allow the skin to dry thoroughly.
- Wear disposable gloves and washable overalls when handling an infected horse.
- Long hair is best clipped away from around scabbed areas if the horse can be given a dry environment. Take care not to further traumatize the skin when clipping around the uneven scabs. Disinfect the clipper blades after use.
- A single application of glucocorticoid spray can reduce local inflammation.
- Antibacterial washes can reduce the bacterial load, but the hard scabs are difficult and uncomfortable to dislodge, and bacteria are protected within them. A gentle washing technique is needed to avoid more trauma to the skin. Warm water washes or compresses will soften and remove a proportion of the scabs. It is essential to dry the skin thoroughly after washing. Kitchen paper is soft and absorbent, and works well with a blotting action as the final drying material.

- Scabs can be cut gently from the hair coat when they have grown out a little, and rounded scissors can be slid underneath the scab. This is not possible in active infections.
- Dispose of dislodged scabs by burning, as they are likely to contain infectious bacteria.
- Antibiotics may be necessary for severe cases. They will kill the bacteria that are invading the skin, but will not kill the bacteria protected within the scabs.

Management Options

- Provide a field shelter for grazing animals to avoid exposure to prolonged or heavy rain.
- Review rugs regularly. Ideally, they keep the horse dry, but do not cause sweating.
- Review the amount of coat, versus the amount of work, a horse is doing. Clip the hair coat accordingly to avoid regular and heavy sweating.
- Clean sweat sheets regularly and do not share them between horses.
- Manage flies. Flies can transmit bacteria from infected sweating horses to the broken skin of another horse.
- Check tack, rugs, harness, grooming kit, stables, fencing, clipper blades, etc., for causes of abrasion and skin damage. Rain scald can only take hold when there is a break in the skin.
- Do not share tack, grooming kit, rugs, etc., with other horses.
- Clean tack, grooming kit, rugs, etc., thoroughly and treat with a suitable antibacterial product.

MUD FEVER COMPLEX (PASTERN DERMATITIS)

The term 'mud fever', like the term 'lameness', describes a clinical condition with a wide range of possible underlying causes. Recognizing mud fever is not a diagnosis, but is the start of a long and labour-intensive search for the particular factors involved in any individual case. Sometimes the term mud fever is used specifically to describe rain scald affecting the pastern area. More commonly, the term is used loosely to describe inflamed skin (dermatitis) of the pastern area. Rain scald is a common cause of mud fever, but other factors may be involved.

Mud fever is listed here under contagious diseases because some underlying causes such as ringworm and rain scald are contagious – however, other causes such as photosensitization are not.

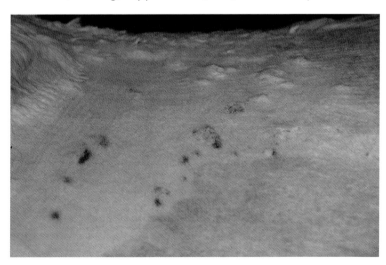

A coloured gelding with rain scald. There are multiple thick scabs over the saddle area. The scabs are tightly adherent to the underlying skin. It is not usually possible to clip out the scabs but, as here, it is useful to clip around them as gently as possible if the horse can be kept dry. Note that the lesions are restricted to the non-pigmented skin. Ultraviolet irradiation suppresses the function of the local immune system in the non-pigmented areas. (Photo: M. Corke)

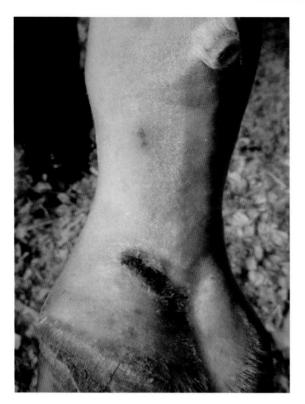

A tightly adherent scab on the back of a white pastern. This lesion was difficult to appreciate until the area was clipped.

POSSIBLE FACTORS INVOLVED IN MUD FEVER COMPLEX

Muddy conditions underfoot
Prolonged wetting of the skin
Abrasion or trauma to the pastern area
Photosensitization
Vasculitis (inflammation of the blood vessels)
Chorioptes mites
Harvest mites
Contact irritation
Contact allergy
Rain scald (*Dermatophilus*) infection
Other bacterial infection, for example with
    Staphylococcus
Ringworm infection

What Mud Fever Looks Like

This condition is most commonly seen in adult draught breeds with feathered legs. White legs are more susceptible than pigmented ones. The back of the pastern, on the hind legs, is the most common location. Early lesions can appear with dry flaking and scabs, or some local inflammation. Chronic severe lesions can progress to involve all of the lower leg, and show significant leg swelling and skin thickening. There may be an associated unpleasant smell.

Causes of Mud Fever

The condition can be triggered by a range of factors, and complicated and perpetuated by other factors. It is helpful to try to find the primary triggers early in the course of the disease. Waiting, and trying a few speculative treatments, usually allows the disease to progress and to become more complicated, both to diagnose and to treat.

Making the Diagnosis

The diagnosis is made by working patiently through the list of possible underlying causes. Samples can be assessed under the microscope for *Dermatophilus*, other types of bacteria and ringworm. Swabs, taken from underneath scabs, may be used to grow and identify bacteria in the laboratory. Samples can be sent away for fungal culture. Skin scraping is helpful to look for *Chorioptes* and harvest mites. Looking at the management history and recent weather conditions will help to assess rainfall or sweating, muddy conditions and skin abrasion, and contact with creams that may be causing irritation or allergic reactions. Blood samples for liver assessment are needed if photosensitization is suspected. Sometimes a skin biopsy is helpful, and is the only way to diagnose vasculitis. Cases of mud fever are likely to be the result of several factors operating together to cause disease.

Treatment Options

- Wear disposable gloves and washable overalls when handling an infected horse, at least until a diagnosis is made of the underlying cause.
- Clip all of the hair away from the affected areas, including from a margin of normal-looking skin. Take care not to further traumatize the skin when clipping around the uneven abnormal areas. Disinfect the clipper blades after use.

- Stable the horse during treatment or provide clean dry standing. Ensure that good-quality bedding is used, and that it is changed regularly, to provide a clean and dry environment. Clean, dry rubber matting is non-abrasive to the pastern and allows good air circulation to the area.
- Warm water washes will soften and remove a proportion of the scabs. Antibacterial washes can reduce the bacterial load. The crusted and scabby areas can be difficult and uncomfortable to dislodge, and bacteria are protected within them. It is not necessary to remove all of the crust and debris at the first attempt. A gentle washing technique is needed to avoid more trauma to the skin. It is essential to dry the skin thoroughly after washing. Kitchen paper is soft and absorbent, and

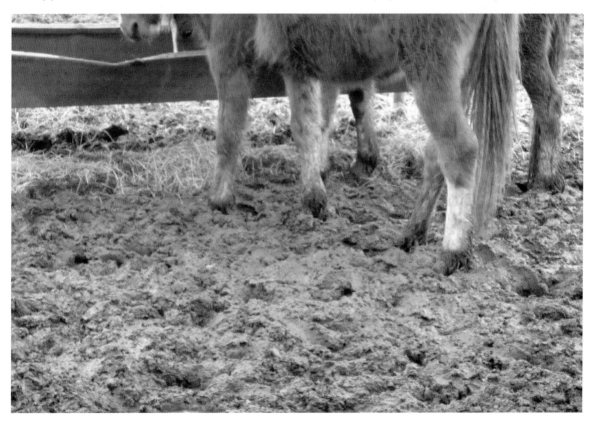

Muddy conditions underfoot, especially around the feed trough.

works well with a blotting action as the final drying material.

- Severely affected and/or sensitive horses may need sedation, with or without local nerve blocks, before the legs are handled.
- Appropriate antibiotics by mouth, if bacteria are known to be involved.
- Antibiotic/steroid creams should be used with caution, and only as part of a rational treatment plan for the lesion.
- Bandages can contribute to a clean and dry leg, but can also cause trauma and keep the skin too humid. The suitability of bandaging depends on the type of dressing used, the type of lesion and how well the bandage is applied.
- Thoroughly clean the grooming kit, boots, etc., and treat them with a suitable antibacterial product.

Management Options

- Manage the pasture to avoid the development of poached, muddy areas. Rotate the areas used for mineral licks, supplementary feeding, etc. Provide hard standing around permanent features such as water troughs. Consider fencing off badly trampled and muddy areas to allow grass to recover. Drain persistently waterlogged areas.
- Avoid exercise over abrasive surfaces such as gravel, and through bracken, gorse, thistles, etc.
- Carefully inspect boots, grooming kit, etc., for cleanliness, and for rough surfaces that may cause skin abrasion.
- Do not share bandages, grooming kit, boots, etc., with other horses.
- Regularly check predisposed individuals for early signs of recurrence.

9 Non-Contagious Skin Diseases

Diseases that are not contagious cannot be passed from one horse to another, even if they are next to each other on a yard, or share the same field. Several horses in a group may be affected with the same thing, for example sunburn, but they are all getting it as a result of sharing a common environment. There is not an infectious agent spreading between the horses.

PEMPHIGUS FOLIACEUS (PF)

PF is the most common autoimmune condition in the horse. In autoimmune disease the immune system reacts against the horse's own tissues. The horse's immune system fails to recognize normal components of the skin as 'self' and attacks them as 'other'.

What PF Looks Like

The condition affects horses of all ages, including foals. Signs commonly begin on the legs and head, but may occur anywhere on the body. The normal tight binding between skin cells is broken down and non-infected blisters, or pustules, develop within the epidermis. Skin pustules rapidly rupture and the dried remnants form crust and scale on the skin surface. The term 'foliaceus' means leaf-like. It refers to the peeling sheets, or leaves, of skin and crust that can be seen in long-standing cases. Raw-looking areas of erosion can be seen if the crusts are dislodged. There is a variable amount of hair loss and redness of the skin. The condition is seldom itchy, but extensive

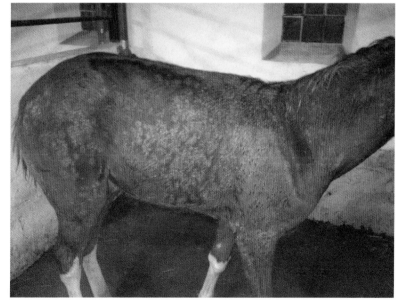

*A five-month-old Arabian foal with **Pemphigus foliaceus**. There is widespread crusting over the entire body, and intermittent fever. The condition is uncomfortable but not itchy. (Photo: G. Pedersen)*

leg lesions, or coronary band involvement, can cause lameness. Occasionally the skin around the ergots, chestnuts and coronary bands can be the only areas affected. Some horses have a raised temperature, lethargy and are off their feed. Others may have filling of the lower legs and swelling of the underside of the body.

PF can, occasionally, be associated with internal neoplastic disease. This form of PF is generally seen in older horses and has a rapid and extensive development of clinical signs.

Making the Diagnosis

The diagnosis is made by ruling out other conditions that cause similar signs, and analysis of biopsies taken from affected areas of skin. It is helpful not to do any skin preparation before taking a biopsy for suspected PF. Clipping or washing of the skin can dislodge surface crust, or damage pustules and vesicles. Pieces of crust and scale often give the histopathological diagnosis and should always be included in the sample pot, even if they become detached from the skin when the biopsies are taken.

Treatment Options

The majority of cases are treated with steroids. These drugs have dose-dependent effects on the body. Daily doses are needed to suppress the immune system, and to bring PF into remission, before the dose is tapered down. Young horses are likely to be able to come off medication, after tapering, and stay in remission. Older horses are likely to need ongoing medication, at individually tailored doses, to keep the disease in remission. Maintenance doses are generally given on alternate days. Alternate- day dosing helps to maintain the ability of the body to produce its own steroids over the long term. Short-acting steroids given by mouth are preferable to

long-acting injectable formulations. The use of steroids carries the risk of inducing laminitis, particularly in horses with pre-existing insulin resistance. Horses at risk of developing laminitis need careful attention to bodyweight, diet, foot care and exercise during their treatment with steroids. Long-acting injectable steroid formulations carry a higher risk of precipitating laminitis, and the steroid action cannot be stopped quickly if signs of laminitis occur.

SUNBURN

The skin is protected against ultraviolet radiation by the physical barrier of the hair coat, the external layer of skin cells and the melanin pigments contained in the skin. The DNA within the nucleus of the cell is especially vulnerable to radiation damage. The protective melanin pigments are arranged as a cap over the cell nucleus to shield the DNA. The energy contained within the sun's rays is highest in the middle of the day, during the summer months and at higher altitudes. Ultraviolet rays penetrate into unprotected skin and damage skin cells, largely by the formation of oxygen-free radicals. Connective tissue and blood vessels can also be damaged. The local immune response is impaired. Reduced local immune function may lead to a bacterial infection of the area.

What Sunburn Looks Like

Sunburn typically occurs on hairless, or thinly haired, areas of skin which have little or no pigmentation – for example, where a white blaze extends towards an eye or a nostril. Scarred areas are also vulnerable as the skin is thin and has often lost its pigment. Horses with areas of hair loss, or with closely clipped hair, are at risk of sunburn.

Sunburned skin is initially red and swollen,

itchy or painful, and may weep tissue fluid, which dries to form a crust. The edge of an area of swollen non-pigmented skin may feel or look raised, when compared to the adjacent pigmented skin. The dead surface skin layer may crack and slough off over time, in severe cases.

Making the Diagnosis

Heat, redness, swelling and discomfort are seen on areas of skin that are poorly protected

Sunburn affecting the face. It is helpful to assess pastures for their shade opportunities at different times of day, especially between 10am and 3pm in the summer, when the ultraviolet light is most damaging. Note that the affected skin has the least pigment.

from the sun. Adjacent well-protected skin will appear normal. Sunburn usually occurs when vulnerable skin is exposed to enough intensity of ultraviolet light for a long enough period. Horses with sunburn, without an obvious cause, may be photosensitized and the reasons for this should be investigated.

Treatment Options

- Anti-inflammatory medication to relieve itching and pain.
- Soothing creams may be helpful on burned skin.
- Dead burned skin may need surgical debridement (see Chapter 11).

Management Options

- Vulnerable areas of skin can be protected with a variety of UV barrier clothing or sunblock creams. These need to be employed at strategic times of the day and year.
- It is useful to pay attention to local weather forecasts that include the predicted levels of ultraviolet radiation.
- Sunburn is best avoided by providing options for shade. It is helpful to be familiar with the behaviour of at-risk animals during sunny periods. A horse may choose to stand in the sunny breeze, away from shady trees, if there is significant fly-worry. A simple shade shelter, built for example of two sides of big bales and a tarpaulin roof, with a breeze funnelling down the open centre, can provide sun protection and relief from flies.

GRANULOMAS

A granuloma is a local tissue reaction that forms around a focus. That focus may be a group of bacteria or fungi in the skin, or it may be some foreign material, such as a thorn or a tick bite. Granulomas usually form slowly and stay for long periods. They contain characteristic types of cells (macrophages). It is often difficult to distinguish the underlying cause of a granuloma without examining material from a tissue biopsy. Fungal hyphae may, for example, be seen in histopathology sections when special stains are used. It is useful, when taking biopsies of granulomas, to take some samples for histopathology and some for bacterial and fungal culture. Taking enough material on the first occasion can avoid the need to return for more samples at a later time.

Eosinophilic Granulomas (Collagenolytic Granulomas)

These are commonly encountered skin nodules. They are not itchy or painful. The skin over them is intact and covered with hair. Eosinophilic granulomas are most often seen over the back and the neck. They start small and are often first noticed when they are felt, rather than seen. Some granulomas grow slowly in size and can reach a few centimetres in diameter. They are firm to the touch and have well-defined edges. Samples taken by fine needle aspirate, or after removal, show that they contain cells typical of granulomas (macrophages), along with eosinophils (another type of white blood cell associated with inflammation). The cause is not understood, but a reaction to insect bites has been suggested. The nodules usually cause no harm and can be left alone. Large nodules, when they occur in problematical places, can be surgically removed.

Subcutaneous Fungal Granulomas

Many different types of fungus are widespread in the environment and can be found on the coat of a horse. Horses in the temperate climate of the UK are largely spared the more aggressive and ulcerating subcutaneous fungal infections caused by organisms such as *Pythium* (pythiosis) or *Sporothrix shenckii* (sporotrichosis). A number of less pathogenic fungi, for example *Alternaria*, cause infrequent problems in the UK. Fungi are able to enter the skin through minor abrasions or fly bite wounds. They establish an infection in the subcutaneous tissues. They are not able to break through intact healthy skin unaided. Individual horses are in contact with fungi in the environment and the condition is not contagious from horse to horse.

Eosinophilic granulomas in the saddle area. The nodules are mostly haired; a few have had the overlying hair abraded away. They have a firm texture. These nodules are approximately 7mm (0.3in) in diameter.

What Subcutaneous Fungal Granulomas Look Like

Fungal granulomas appear as firm, rounded nodules in the skin. The nodules start small and increase slowly in size. They grow up to about 1cm (0.4in) in diameter. There is variable hair loss over, or immediately around, the nodules. Most nodules do not cause itching or pain. They can occur at any site on the body.

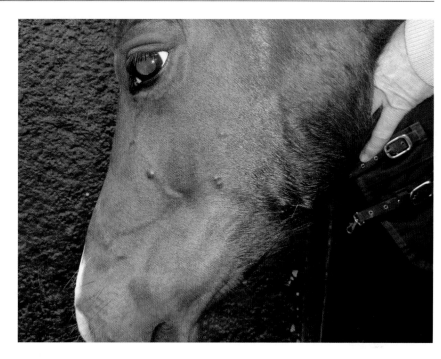

*This ten-year-old mare had about twenty darkly pigmented, firm, raised nodules all over her face. The number of nodules had increased, from one to twenty, over the past four months. Biopsy of the nodules showed fragments of plant material and fungal granulomas in the skin. Culture from a biopsy grew **Alternaria**, a fungus that is widespread in the environment.*
(Photo: J. Dukes)

Treatment Options

- Fungal granulomas, when found at a body site where they do not interfere with the tack and do not risk abrasion, may be left untreated and monitored periodically.
- Surgical removal is best done with a good margin, as the granuloma is likely to re-form if some fungal material is left in the skin.
- Potassium iodide, given as a medication by mouth, can give variable degrees of improvement.

MALASSEZIA DERMATITIS

Malassezia pachydermatis is a type of yeast. It can be found in low numbers on the skin of normal horses with no skin problems. Yeast numbers can increase when the local microclimate is favourable, such as in warm and damp folds of skin. The most common area for *Malassezia* dermatitis is in the midline fold between the mammary glands of mares. Dark-coloured greasy debris can accumulate in this area and cause irritation. The area is difficult for mares to scratch directly and most will rub their rump and tail to gain some relief from the irritation. The insides of the elbows and prepuce are occasionally affected, and *Malassezia* can be a complicating factor in pastern dermatitis.

Making the Diagnosis

Malassezia has a characteristic appearance under the microscope. The yeasts are easily stained with methylene blue stain and have a dumpy round to oval appearance. They are very small (3–8microns in diameter) and are best

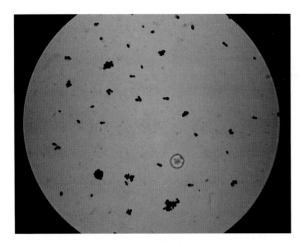

This photograph was taken through a microscope. It shows the rounded peanut-shaped yeasts called Malassezia. *The yeasts are stained purple to make them easier to see.*

seen using the ×100 oil immersion microscope lens. We expect to see high numbers of *Malassezia* in clinical cases. Low numbers are considered normal.

The yeasts can be collected by pushing clear acetate tape onto the affected area, or by making a superficial scraping with a wooden spatula. Care is needed when sampling the area between the mammary glands as it may be sore and sensitive. Sedation may be needed for both sampling and subsequent cleaning of the area.

Treatment Options

- Gently and thoroughly remove the greasy debris from between the mammary glands.
- Wash the area with an anti-*Malassezia* product, for example miconazole and/or chlorhexidine. Rinse and dry well. Blotting with kitchen paper is helpful at the end, to leave the skin dry.
- Recurrence after treatment is variable. Recurrent cases can be managed with strategic debris removal and anti-yeast creams or washes.

HEREDITARY EQUINE REGIONAL DERMAL ASTHENIA (HERDA)

This is a hereditary disease which affects Quarter Horses, Appaloosas and American Paints. It was first reported in horses in 1978, and is thought to have arisen as a genetic mutation in a popular Quarter Horse stallion in the 1940s. Horses with only one copy of the affected gene (N/Hrd) do not have skin lesions, but they pass the affected gene on to their offspring. The affected gene creates abnormally loose and disorganized connective tissue in the skin, but also in the cornea, the tendons and ligaments, major blood vessels and heart valves. Some affected horses have abnormally flexible joints.

What HERDA Looks Like

Horses affected with HERDA look normal when they are born. They have two copies of the affected gene (Hrd/Hrd). Problems are usually noticed in young adults of one and a half to two years of age. Some horses only show signs as mature adults of four to six years of age, often associated with putting on a saddle. The skin can appear soft, pliable and more loosely attached than normal. It is able to be stretched away from the body in folds. Loose skin areas may slough spontaneously, leaving open wounds, or the skin may tear easily following only a minimal amount of trauma. Wounds often heal slowly, with the formation of permanent scarring. Some horses form large swellings of accumulated blood or serum under the skin. Clinical signs appear to be more severe in the presence of high sunlight levels, and occur most frequently over the back. The extent and severity of clinical signs varies widely between affected animals. Some affected horses show only a few mild lesions, while others are severely affected.

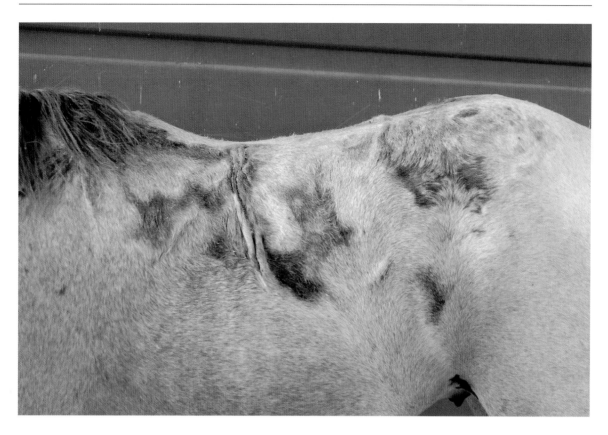

A two-year-old Quarter Horse with HERDA, showing typical scarring over the back. (Photo: A. Rashmir Raven)

Making the Diagnosis

A horse of an affected breed, with suggestive clinical signs, can be tested to see if the affected gene (Hrd) is present. Genetic testing can be performed on DNA extracted from hair samples. About forty mane or tail hairs are needed, not cut hairs but ones pulled out with their roots intact.

Management Options

There is no treatment for the disease. Skin fragility often prevents affected horses from being ridden. As they are also unsuitable as breeding stock, many are euthanized at a young age. Affected individuals used for breeding should only be crossed with stock not carrying the Hrd gene (N/N in genetic testing). Mildly affected horses need careful management, as follows.

- Avoid intense sunlight.
- Minimize trauma to the skin and eyes.
- Optimize the healing of any wounds that occur.
- Dietary supplementation with vitamin C, glucosamine, chondroitin and lysine may be of benefit.

CONTACT IRRITATION

This condition results in inflammation of the skin and may appear as redness, swelling, weeping fluid and variable itching of the affected area. There is usually a history of direct contact with an irritant. The clinical signs are similar to a contact allergy, the only difference being that irritation can occur at the first exposure and does not need a period of sensitization. Contact irritation is likely to affect the whole group of horses exposed to the same material, whereas contact allergy is likely only to affect a single allergic individual. Contact irritation has been reported, for example, to certain bedding materials, scalding by urine and faeces, the application of motor oil as a totally unsuitable fly repellent, and accidental contact with some wood preservatives. Some plants may be irritant, such as stinging nettles (*Urtica*) and the sap of spurge (*Euphorbia*). Strongly alkaline substances, such as cement powder, can also cause skin irritation. Inflammation of the skin is only seen in the areas corresponding to direct contact with the problematical material. Contact irritation can be treated by washing the affected area with lots of water and a very mild shampoo in order to dilute and remove any remaining irritating material. Marked inflammation, especially if associated with itching and self-trauma, can be treated by the short-term application of corticosteroid cream or spray to the affected area. The irritating agent should be avoided, as much as possible, in the future.

10 Changes in the Skin and Coat that Point Towards Internal Disease

HIRSUTISM

Hirsutism is the presence of a long, dense and often curly hair coat that is not shed with the normal seasonal pattern. The retained hair may become pale-coloured in some individuals, especially over the trunk. The mane and tail appear normal. Hirsutism, when present, is characteristic of pituitary pars intermedia dysfunction (PPID), also known as equine Cushing's disease. Not all horses with PPID will have this appearance: the degree of hirsutism can vary. Some horses have discrete areas of the body with retained hair, and an uneven appearance to the coat. Others have a shaggy coat that is retained all year round. Some horses with PPID have more subtle signs, with delayed shedding each year. These horses will retain their winter coat longer than other horses that share the same environment. The characteristic shaggy, sweaty appearance of the coat may be missed if an affected horse is regularly clipped out.

The pituitary gland lies at the base of the brain and the pars intermedia is its middle layer. When this layer of the pituitary is overactive, there is an excessive production of certain hormones, including adrenocorticotrophic hormone (ACTH) and melanocyte stimulating hormone (MSH). ACTH acts on the adrenal glands to stimulate the release of corticosteroids. Increased activity of the pars intermedia is thought to result from falling dopamine levels in ageing horses. Dopamine normally has an inhibitory effect on the pars intermedia. A benign but productive tumour, a pituitary adenoma, may be responsible for an overactive pars intermedia in younger horses.

What PPID Looks Like

Individual horses will show different combinations of clinical signs. The clinical signs can vary from mild to severe. The condition usually occurs in horses over fifteen years of age and rarely affects those younger than ten. The onset of clinical signs is gradual. This gradual onset is typical of most hormonal conditions. Ponies are more commonly affected than horses.

Making the Diagnosis

A diagnosis is achieved by assessing the clinical signs, ruling out other possible causes of those signs, and assessing the results of special blood tests for PPID.

Horses with PPID need regular monitoring and care. It can be helpful to keep a diary, or spreadsheet, of events and findings. Features such as appetite, lameness, demeanour, water intake, how wet the bedding is, and a bodyweight or condition score can all be useful

CLINICAL SIGNS OF PPID

Hirsutism

Excessive sweating, especially over the neck and shoulders

Weight loss

Lethargy

Increased appetite

Body fat accumulation over the crest, above the eye (supraorbital fossa), and tail head

Muscle wasting, especially over the back

Laminitis

Increased susceptibility to infection, for example in the teeth, skin, respiratory tract or feet

Increased susceptibility to internal and external parasites

Slow wound healing

Excessive drinking and urination

Absence of reproductive cycles/infertility

Management Options

- Coat clipping, as appropriate to the season of the year.
- Hoof care, with awareness of possible infections and/or laminitis.
- Keep routine vaccinations up to date.
- Weight control by optimum nutrition. PPID is associated with insulin resistance and increased laminitis risk, so a low sugar and low starch diet is helpful. Underweight horses, however, need enough calories; they may benefit from added fat in the diet.
- Parasite control – consider both internal and external parasites.
- Appropriate exercise. Horses with PPID have a degree of insulin resistance and will benefit from regular exercise to help regulate their blood sugar levels. This needs to be balanced against any orthopaedic issues in an older horse, and any active laminitis.
- Good dental care.

information. Trends in this information allow the response to treatment to be monitored, and any emerging issues to be identified. Our memories are often unreliable and it is helpful to record this sort of information regularly, with an associated date.

Treatment Options

Treatment does not stop the slow progression of the disease. However, treated horses can show a significant improvement in their quality of life, and a marked reduction in their clinical signs. There is no cure for PPID, so treatment needs to be continued for the rest of the horse's life.

The following drugs may be used in the treatment of PPID.

An elderly horse with pituitary pars intermedia disease (PPID). The coat is long and curly, with a shaggy appearance. (Photo: P. Green)

Pergolide is the first treatment choice and is the only licensed treatment option for PPID in the UK. It is effective for between 65 and 80 per cent of cases at the standard dose. Pergolide binds to dopamine receptors in the body. It acts as a replacement for the falling dopamine levels in ageing horses with PPID. Studies have shown pergolide to be more effective than cyproheptadine.

Cyproheptadine is a type of antihistamine. It is less effective than pergolide, but can be added to pergolide in severe cases.

Bromocryptine is given daily by mouth. An improvement in clinical signs, for example shedding some of the heavy coat, is usually evident within two weeks if the treatment is going to work.

Trilostane is a drug that suppresses the part of the adrenal gland that makes corticosteroids. It is licensed for Cushing's disease in dogs. However, since the disease is not the same in dogs as in horses, the efficacy of trilostane in the horse is unclear.

Laminitis and/or secondary infections should be treated as appropriate.

The prognosis depends on the severity of clinical signs, the quantity and quality of available management care, and the response to medication. Horses without, for example, severe laminitis or weight loss can be maintained for several years with a good quality of life.

MULTISYSTEMIC EOSINOPHILIC EPITHELIOTROPHIC DISEASE (MEED)

This is a rare condition. It most commonly, but not exclusively, affects young adult horses.

Eosinophils, plasma cells and lymphocytes are white blood cells associated with the horse's immune response. In MEED these white blood cells move into multiple organs of the body. They form diffuse infiltrates and accumulate to form clusters (granulomas). The liver, intestine, kidneys, pancreas and lungs can be affected, along with the skin. The cause of this widespread cell infiltration, into multiple organs, is poorly understood at present.

Early signs are scaling of the skin and weeping of exudate, which dries to form crusts. There may be multiple nodules, or lines of thickened skin. The coronary bands, muzzle, legs and mouth are commonly affected. These early signs may be interpreted as abrasions or, on the legs, as mud fever. The skin signs become steadily more extensive and progress to erosion, ulceration, cracking and hair loss. The hair of the mane and tail may fall out. There is a variable – up to severe – amount of itchiness, some of which may be a response to a concurrent bacterial skin infection.

The infiltration of internal organs may give signs of weight loss despite a good appetite. Loose stools, colic and an intermittently raised body temperature can also occur. Note, however, that horses often appear to be bright and well in the early stages of the disease.

The diagnosis is made by taking biopsy samples of skin, and possibly rectal tissue, and sending them to a histopathologist for analysis. Ultrasound examination of the abdomen may show thickened loops of small intestine.

The prognosis is generally poor, with a deterioration in clinical signs progressing over time. Treatment with immunosuppressive doses of corticosteroids has led to an improvement of the clinical signs in some cases.

GENERALIZED GRANULOMATOUS DISEASE (SARCOIDOSIS)

This is another rare condition, and the two may be related. Clusters of inflammatory cells

SOME EXAMPLES OF CAUSES OF PHOTOSENSITIZATION

Primary Photosensitization	Photodynamic Agent
St John's Wort (*Hypericum*)	Hypericin
Tetracycline antibiotics	Unknown

Secondary Photosensitization	
Ragwort (*Senecio*)	Phylloerythrin (accumulates in liver failure)

(granulomas) accumulate in the tissues of the skin, liver, kidneys, lungs and/or the intestines. 'Generalized' in the name of the disease refers to the wide variety of organs that are involved. 'Granulomatous' refers to the formation of granulomas in these organs. Individual horses will have different organs that are more affected. The condition presents with a range of clinical signs, usually including weight loss. The most striking sign can be obvious crusting and scaling over large areas of the skin, and/or multiple skin nodules.

The cause of this condition is not presently understood. Theories include an inappropriate response by the horse's immune system, to some undetermined allergen, in individuals with a genetic predisposition. The term sarcoidosis, an alternative name for the disease, is easily confused with the unrelated neoplastic skin lesions called sarcoids and so may be best avoided.

Treatment with immunosuppressive doses of steroids has led to an improvement of the clinical signs in some cases. Some cases spontaneously wax and wane in severity.

PHOTOSENSITIZATION

Photosensitization looks just like sunburn. However, while sunburn is associated with high levels of exposure to ultraviolet light, signs of photosensitization can occur after relatively low levels of exposure to ultraviolet radiation.

The unique factor with photosensitization is the presence of photodynamic agents, which pass to the skin in the bloodstream. These photodynamic agents absorb the energy of

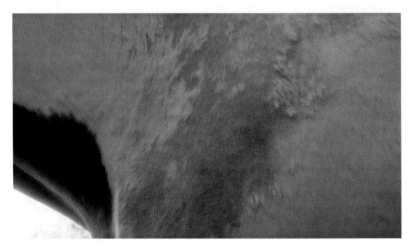

A coloured gelding with photosensitization and underlying hepatitis. The cause of the hepatitis was not known. There is redness, inflammation and hair loss on the non-pigmented areas of skin. Note that the pigmented skin, to the left of the picture, has a normal appearance.

ultraviolet light and amplify its destructive effect on the skin. They all produce a sunburn-type outcome, which is more severe than would be anticipated for the degree of sun exposure received. Photodynamic agents can come from a wide range of sources.

Primary photosensitization occurs in horses with a healthy liver. Certain plants contain photodynamic pigments and, if eaten in sufficient quantity, they can trigger photosensitization. For example the common native plant St John's Wort (*Hypericum perforatum*) contains the photoactive pigment hypericin.

Ragwort

This common weed contains a number of alkaloids, which are damaging to the liver. Fresh ragwort has a bitter taste and is unpalatable to horses, but dried ragwort is more palatable and may be eaten in enough quantity to be damaging to the liver. Dried ragwort can, mistakenly, be incorporated into hay.

Ragwort toxicity is an example of secondary, or liver-based, photosensitization. The photosensitization is secondary to the liver damage. (Other, non-ragwort, causes of liver damage can give similar outcomes.)

The ragwort plant grows taller, and has flowers, in its second year. This plant is approximately 1m (3.25ft) tall. It is growing in a typical unmown rough grassland location.

The ragwort plant has a lifecycle that takes two years. This rosette of leaves, which is flat to the ground, is produced in the first year.

Ragwort flowers are bright yellow in colour. They have many petals surrounding a darker centre.

DESCRIPTION AND MANAGEMENT OF RAGWORT

Ragwort (*Senecio*) is a plant with a two-year lifecycle. The first year has a rosette of leaves close to the ground. In the second year the plant can grow up to 2m (6.5ft) tall. It produces bright yellow flowers at the top of a straight, sturdy stem. The flowers are about 2cm (0.8in) across. They have approximately thirteen pointed petals, radiating out from a round yellow centre. The leaves are dark green on top, and paler below, with a ragged appearance. Ragwort is in the same plant family (*Compositae*) as dandelions and thistles. Like them, it produces a large number of fluffy seeds after flowering, which are spread on the wind. Ragwort is a common wildflower of open spaces. It is frequently seen beside roads and on wasteland. It is native to Europe and Asia, and has been widely introduced to many countries around the world.

Mowing is not a good way of controlling ragwort as the plant will re-grow from the remaining stump, and the cut dried plant material may be eaten by horses. Ragwort plants should be pulled up with the roots attached, or treated with an appropriate weed killer.

The liver of a healthy horse breaks down phylloerythrin, which comes from the chlorophyll in green plants. When a horse has a damaged liver, phylloerythrin can accumulate in the blood. Phylloerythrin is a photodynamic agent; it causes the signs of photosensitization which are seen with many cases of ragwort poisoning.

Other signs of ragwort poisoning are also associated with liver failure. They include impaired blood clotting, yellow mucous membranes, filling of the legs, and neurological signs such as head-pressing and depression.

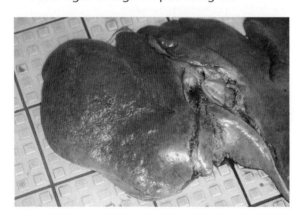

The liver from a mare euthanized because of ragwort toxicity. The mare had marked photosensitization on her white nose and socks, and bleeding from one nostril. She was found head-pressing in the corner of her field. The liver is smaller than normal and has a coppery colour.

Management Options

- Identify the cause of the photosensitization. All cases need liver evaluation.
- Remove or avoid the cause to prevent further damage.
- Manage the pasture to control ragwort and other known toxic plants.
- Avoid sunlight, or protect the skin from sunlight.

Treatment Options

- Control skin inflammation and pain.
- Treat underlying liver pathology, if present.
- Assess for secondary bacterial infection and treat if present.
- Dead sloughing skin may need surgical removal.

11 Wounds and Wound Healing

Traumatic wounds are common in horses and come in many forms. Kicks and bites, a leg down a cattle grid or through a partition, overreaching, and tangling with barbed wire all spring readily to mind. Our discussion here will focus on traumatic skin wounds. It is useful to remember that visible skin wounds are often accompanied by less visible damage to underlying muscles, tendons, bones and/or joints, and may be attached to a shocked or sick horse. It is important to assess the whole animal before focusing on the obvious wound. Probing the wound, X-ray pictures and ultrasound examination may be needed to understand the extent and depth of the damage.

Wound healing is a very metabolically active process. The wound needs a constant supply of oxygen and nutrition, which is dependent on an effective blood supply to the skin and enough good-quality nutrients in the diet.

Superficial wounds, for example shallow grazes and scrapes, heal by multiplication and upward migration of the intact epithelial cells that remain at the base of the wound. The trauma only removes some of the surface epidermal layers. The lowest regenerative (basal) layer, and the basement membrane

on which it sits, remain intact. Epithelial cells can also move in from remaining sweat and sebaceous glands, and from hair follicles, to fill the deficit.

Deeper wounds cut through the whole of the epidermis, into the dermis and sometimes beyond. They have a slower and more complex healing process, which can be thought of in a number of stages.

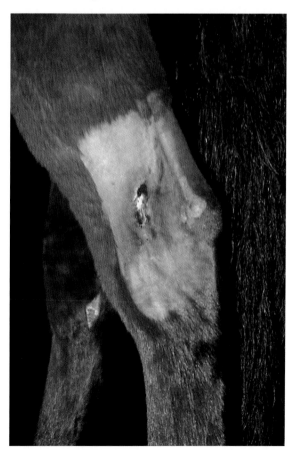

A puncture wound on the left hock. The wound is small but has penetrated deeply and caused infection of the underlying structures.

STAGES OF WOUND HEALING

What follows is a simplified version of the many closely integrated processes involved in wound healing. In reality there is overlap between the three stages described – the inflammatory, proliferative and remodelling phases.

The Inflammatory Phase

Blood, or weeping tissue fluid, coagulates and forms a clot both in and over the wound. The clot plugs the wound and stops further bleeding or weeping. The surface of the clot dries to form a scab. The scab shields the underlying tissue from drying out and from further infection. If a wound is clean, and is not going to be dressed, the scab can be left in place to act as a natural wound covering. Neutrophils, a type of white blood cell, start to move into the clot within hours of the damage occurring. They clean up the wound by engulfing bacteria and debris, and their numbers peak after one to two days. Macrophages, another type of white blood cell, also move into the wound. They

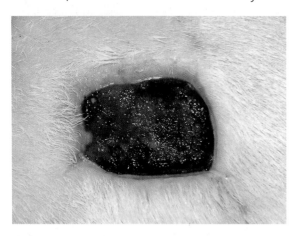

A large wound, with healthy granulation tissue, on the flank of a donkey. The surface has a rough appearance and the colour is bright red, reflecting the excellent blood supply. A narrow rim of pale-pink new surface skin cells can be seen around the edge of the wound. (Photo: A. Thiemann)

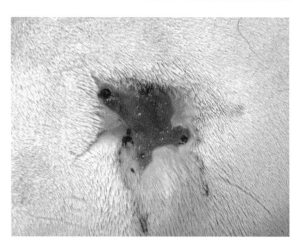

The same flank wound two months later. There has been a significant amount of wound contraction. The pale-pink margin of new surface skin cells is more obvious. (Photo: A. Thiemann)

break down and remove damaged tissue and engulf bacteria. Macrophages release chemical messages that move the wound into the next, proliferative, phase. The inflammatory phase lasts for several days.

The crucial early inflammatory phase can be inhibited by anti-inflammatory drugs. Systemic corticosteroids are known to reduce wound healing and are best avoided. Topical corticosteroids can be helpful over short periods. The non-steroidal anti-inflammatory drugs have not been shown to cause problems over short periods, and can be helpful for pain relief.

The Proliferative Phase

The term 'proliferative' refers here to the infiltration and proliferation of blood vessels, fibroblasts and epithelial cells at the wound site. This proliferation of different cell types is stimulated by chemical messages sent out by the macrophages. The clot of the inflammatory phase is replaced by bright red, fleshy granulation tissue. The bright red colour is a consequence of the rich network of new blood vessels. The word granulation refers to the roughened granular appearance of the surface.

Fibroblasts

Fibroblasts are tissue cells that manufacture the connective tissue framework of the deeper skin layers. They move into the wound, increase in number and produce connective tissue. Their intense metabolic activity is supported by oxygen and nutrients from the new blood vessels. The collagen framework, produced by the fibroblasts, increases the strength of the wound, particularly during the second week after injury. A proportion of the fibroblasts in the wound take on special properties that allow them to shorten in length. By arranging themselves across the wound, attaching to the connective tissue framework and shortening, they can cause the edges of the wound to draw together and the size of the wound to contract. Wound contraction starts one to two weeks after the initial damage and continues for several weeks. It reduces the surface area that needs to be covered by new epithelial cells and reduces the amount of tissue that requires long-term remodelling. Contraction can only happen if the surrounding skin is loose enough to move. Skin over the lower legs and over parts of the head is relatively immobile and resists wound contraction. A wound on the lower legs may contract at 0.2mm every day, in comparison to a wound on the trunk, which may reduce by 0.8mm each day.

Epithelial Cells

Epithelial cells at the edge of the wound move in to cover over the granulation tissue. Before moving they loosen their attachments to their neighbours and to the underlying basement membrane. The rate of movement of epithelial cells over granulation tissue is very variable. Movement is usually slowest over leg skin that is furthest from the body. One millimetre of new epithelium is likely to form in five days for a flank wound, but the same amount of epithelium may take eleven days to form for a wound on a lower limb. In contrast to the bright red granulation tissue, the advancing edge of new epithelial cells has a delicate pale-pink colour and a relatively smooth surface. It can usually be seen as a new pink band about two weeks after the initial wound occurred.

A moist, warm, clean environment gives the best conditions for new epithelial cells to migrate. The proliferative phase starts after a few days, and extends up to several weeks after the wound occurred.

The Remodelling Phase

Granulation tissue, covered by a layer of epithelial cells, will provide rapid and essential protection for the body, but it is structurally inferior to the adjacent normal skin. A lot of wound reorganization takes place in the remodelling phase. The reorganization occurs over a long timeframe of months to years, to create a more robust and functional area of skin. The collagen framework, which was initially made by the fibroblasts, tends to have a random arrangement of fibres. As remodelling progresses, the framework gains fibres orientated along the lines of stress on the wound. There is also increased cross-linking between the fibres. The remodelled arrangement is much more resilient than a freshly healed wound, but is never as strong as the original tissue. A remodelling wound has about half the strength of normal tissue after three months. The final healed wound will have approximately 80 per cent of the strength of the original undamaged tissue. The layer of epithelial cells that migrates over the granulation tissue settles down, attaches to the deeper tissues, and divides to form a new multi-layered epidermis.

We can imagine the degree of co-ordination required for these three complex processes to happen in the right order, and to just the right degree. In an individual wound there is overlap between the three phases. Some areas, within the same wound, may progress at different rates from other areas. Perhaps it is more surprising that so many wounds heal well, than that a proportion of wounds have problems.

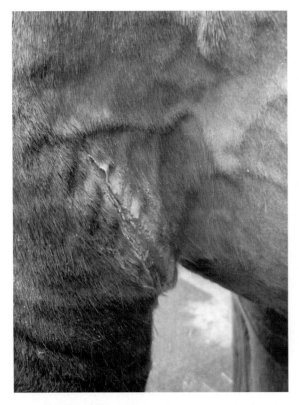

A wound behind the elbow, with mild associated swelling. This horse has been abraded by a piece of poorly fitting tack.

WOUND BREAKDOWN

Wounds that have been surgically closed, or have started to heal by themselves, can sometimes open up again with so-called wound breakdown or dehiscence. Many factors can contribute to wound breakdown. Common factors are too much tension across the wound, too much movement in the area, or infection in the wound. Pony wounds appear to heal faster than wounds on horses, and are also less prone to breakdown.

Early wound breakdown may be a sign of a sarcoid developing at the wound site. This is more likely when a horse already has sarcoids anywhere on the body. Spontaneous skin sloughing, or easily torn skin in Quarter Horses or related breeds, should raise the possibility of hereditary equine regional dermal asthenia (HERDA) being present.

Causes of Wound Breakdown

Too Much Tension

Pulling the wound edges together under too much tension, using sutures (stitches) or staples, is likely to result in wound breakdown. The wound edges are ideally brought together so that they lie alongside one another and are in contact. It is unhelpful for the wound to be so tightly sutured that the tissues are rammed together. The edges need to be held steadily enough to avoid being pulled apart by the elastic recoil of the surrounding tissues. A variety of techniques are available to mobilize the skin and to reduce tension on the wound edges. Skin grafting can also be considered.

Too Much Movement

Movement of the sutured area causes shear forces across the wound edges, which are attempting to fuse together, and disrupts the healing attempt. The newly formed tissue in the wound is not as robust as the surrounding structures and it will be the weak point that shears. The wound edges need to have the least possible movement, relative to each

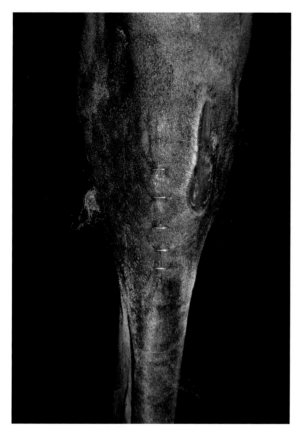

A vertical wound, twenty-four hours after surgery, on the back of the hock. The skin has been held together with the minimal amount of tension or movement, to give the best chance of wound healing. Five stainless steel staples are stabilizing the skin.

other, when the horse moves around. This requirement has led to the successful use of casts to immobilize wounds in very mobile areas, such as over knees.

Wound Infection

Wounds are likely to become infected if there is a long time delay before they are closed, if the level of contamination is high and if the cleaning attempt before surgical closure is not sufficiently rigorous. Damaged soft tissue, for example from a crush injury or a kick, is poorly equipped to deal with infection. Dead

and dying tissue, as well as the presence of foreign material, increases the likelihood of wound infection. Other factors include the age and general health of the horse. Elderly horses tend to heal more slowly than young adults. Individuals with pituitary pars intermedia dysfunction regularly show slow rates of wound healing, and recurrent infections.

If there is not good tissue to tissue contact through the whole length and depth of the wound, the free spaces can fill with tissue fluid and blood. Fluid-filled pockets increase the likelihood of wound infection. It is important to minimize the amount of dead space in a wound by careful suturing, or by using drains to remove fluid pockets. We saw earlier that most of the cleaning up of bacteria and dead tissue is done by neutrophils and macrophages in the first inflammatory phase of wound healing. Infection occurs when the number of bacteria in the wound overwhelms the ability of the inflammatory cells to neutralize them. Ponies have been shown to have a faster and more active inflammatory phase than horses, which may explain their reduced incidence of wound infection and of wound breakdown.

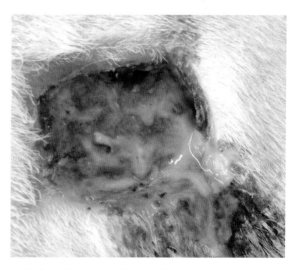

An infected wound. There is a lot of gelatinous green pus on the surface of the wound, and drying to form crust around and below the wound.

TYPES OF WOUND MORE LIKELY TO BECOME INFECTED

- Old wounds, especially those where more than eight hours has passed since the injury occurred.
- Puncture wounds, for example from a nail or stake, can carry bacteria deep into the skin and close over quickly. This allows bacteria to flourish and reduces natural drainage. These cases also have an increased risk of developing tetanus, from the bacterium *Clostridium tetani*.*
- Crush injuries, and de-gloving injuries of the legs, damage and disrupt the local blood supply. With crush injuries the obvious wound is often smaller than the extent of the damaged area.
- Dirty wounds, especially those contaminated with faeces or soil, are at much higher risk of becoming infected. Both faeces and soil contain very high concentrations of bacteria and organic material.
- Wounds containing foreign material, for example plant fragments, will act as a focus of infection.

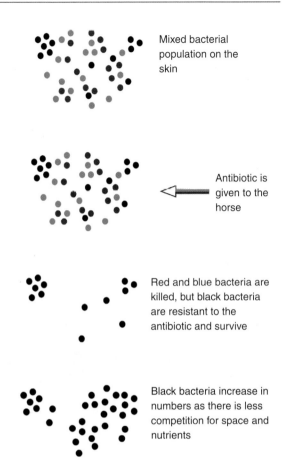

Mixed bacterial population on the skin

Antibiotic is given to the horse

Red and blue bacteria are killed, but black bacteria are resistant to the antibiotic and survive

Black bacteria increase in numbers as there is less competition for space and nutrients

How the use of an antibiotic can select for resistant bacteria.

* Wound infection with *Clostridium tetani* can have disastrous consequences. The toxins produced by the bacteria can cause tetanus. Horses that are not covered by vaccination, or which have an uncertain vaccine history, should be given an injection of tetanus antitoxin.

ANTIBIOTICS

Antibiotics can inhibit or kill bacteria in a wound. They can also inhibit or kill beneficial bacteria in other parts of the body, and create reservoirs of surviving bacteria that are antibiotic resistant. Fresh, superficial and clean wounds generally do not need antibiotics as long as they are carefully clipped and flushed, then sutured and/or dressed.

Antibiotics, if required, are best given as soon as possible after wounding has occurred. They should always be given before a new wound is created, for example before surgical cleaning of a wound, or before cutting back proud flesh. It is best if antibiotics reach their peak concentrations in the body tissues at the time of surgery. For an antibiotic like potassium penicillin this means giving a dose intravenously within an hour of the start of surgery, and repeating it after two hours if the surgery is still ongoing.

Wounds that have been thoroughly and logically treated, but have a persistent bacterial infection, may contain bacteria that are resistant to antibiotics. Such wounds should be sampled to culture some of the bacteria, and to test which antibiotics they are sensitive to. Bacteria may be resistant to a few, or to all, of the antibiotics available. Bacterial culture and sensitivity testing, as well as guiding our choice of treatment, can help us to understand where the infection may have come from, and to address the situation as a whole.

Antibiotics are likely to inhibit, or kill, only a proportion of the bacteria in a wound. The horse's healthy immune system is needed to clear up the dead and impaired bacteria, and to take on the remaining viable population. Any wound with very high bacterial numbers is likely to become infected, even when antibiotics and a healthy immune system are in place. The best way to avoid wound infection is with thorough wound cleaning at an early stage.

> **QUESTIONS TO CONSIDER BEFORE TREATING A WOUND**
>
> - Is there dead or dying tissue in the wound?
> - Is there material from the environment in the wound?
> - Is the wound infected?
> - Is the wound too mobile?
> - How best can the wound be closed?
> - Is the wound best bandaged or left unbandaged?
> - What is the most helpful dressing to apply?

surface, as they will damage exposed cells. Chlorhexidine surgical scrub is not safe in eyes and should not be used anywhere with a risk of running or splashing into an eye. Surgical scrubs should be rinsed thoroughly from the skin.

CLEANING A WOUND

Clipping and Cleaning the Surrounding Skin

Clipping removes a lot of potential contamination and allows the wound edges to be easily seen and assessed. It is helpful to clip a wide area of hair down to the skin and away from the wound edges. The surface of the wound needs to be protected with a physical barrier during clipping, or it will become seriously contaminated by cut hairs. The clipped skin around the wound can be washed with antiseptic and rinsed. Surgical scrub formulations of povodine iodine or chlorhexidine are useful for cleansing the skin. Surgical scrub formulations contain detergent and should not be used on the wound

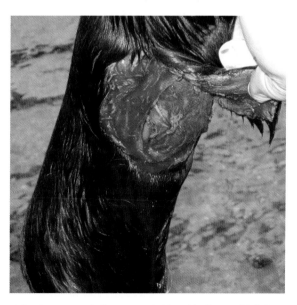

A fresh traumatic leg wound. The skin flap, which has contracted, is lifted to the right to show the depth of the damage to the underlying tissues.

Flushing

Flushing the wound is very important: 'The solution to pollution is dilution.' Flushing is an effective and non-traumatic way of removing bacteria, soil, plant material, loose tissue fragments and faecal material. Tap water running slowly from a hosepipe and a salt water solution are good first aid measures for removing gross contamination from a fresh wound. Attaching a clean shower head to a hosepipe can also be useful. Research has shown that a water pressure of between 7 and 15psi (pounds per square inch), delivered from a side angle, gives the most effective balance between dislodging material and not driving fluid into the wound. This level of pressure can be achieved with a hand-pumped spray bottle, or with a 30ml syringe and a 19-gauge needle. The current understanding is that the most helpful flush solution is 0.9 per cent saline. This concentration of salt water is similar to the salinity of body fluids. In contrast, tap water is much less salty than body fluids and can be harmful to some of the wound repair cells. Tap water is, however, better than nothing as a first aid measure. Wounds can be flushed with an antiseptic solution of povodine iodine or chlorhexidine, diluted with sterile saline. The temptation to add a random unmeasured amount of antiseptic to fluids for flushing should be resisted. Low concentrations of antiseptic are less effective at killing bacteria and high concentrations can reduce the rate of wound healing. The final flush is best done with 0.9 per cent saline.

A commercial wound-flushing device designed to deliver large volumes of fluid at an appropriate pressure. The device is lightweight, portable and robust.

WOUND-FLUSHING SOLUTIONS

A salt water solution can be made with 9g (1.5 teaspoons) of salt in 1 litre (1.75 pints) of body temperature water. Take care that the mixing arrangement for the salt water is very clean. A dirty watering can, stirred with a stick, will not produce the cleansing solution needed.

A 0.2 per cent solution of povodine iodine is made by adding 20ml (non-detergent formulation) to 1 litre of fluid (water/saline).

A 0.05 per cent solution of chlorhexidine is made by adding 25ml of 2 per cent chlorhexidine (non-detergent formulation) to 975ml of fluid.

Debridement

Debridement is the removal of dead and dying tissue, bacteria and foreign material, which cannot be removed from a wound by flushing alone.

Bacteria can be flushed from the surface of fresh wounds, but as time passes bacteria move

A wound on the right shoulder, half a day old. The wound goes through the full thickness of the skin. The triangular skin flap has contracted and stuck down. There is moderate swelling around the wound and some fluid running down the leg. The surface of the wound has dried. The wound will need debridement before it is closed. This horse was kicked by another horse sharing the same field.

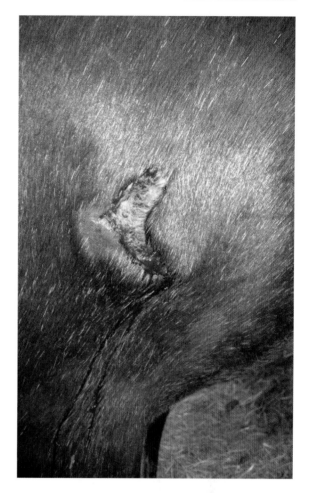

into the tissues. Older wounds will benefit from debridement, for example when more than eight hours has passed since the original damage. It is helpful to debride wounds that have embedded material that is resistant to flushing.

Methods of Debridement
Autolytic Debridement
The body's own wound fluid has a debriding effect. It contains lots of helpful enzymes and white blood cells, which act on dead and devitalized tissue. Keeping appropriate amounts of wound fluid at the wound surface creates a favourable moist healing environment.

Sharp Debridement
Sharp debridement essentially creates a new wound, with better conditions for healing. This can be done with a scalpel blade, with a cutting laser beam or with a pressurized jet of sterile water from a suction and lavage device. These techniques rely on the visual discrimination of the surgeon to guide the cutting, until only healthy tissue is left. The aim is to leave all of the healthy living tissues intact and undamaged.

Dressings
Dressings can be used for debridement. Sterile gauze swabs, wetted with sterile saline solution, can be applied directly to the wound surface and bandaged in place. The swabs are removed while still wet ('wet-to-wet' dressing), or are allowed to dry in the wound ('wet-to-dry' dressing). When the swabs are pulled away from the wound surface they lift with them dried exudate, along with foreign material and bacteria. This can be repeated until the wound bed appears clean, but should not be repeated more than necessary as it is also disruptive to the healing attempt. Wet-to-dry debridement is more traumatic to the wound bed than wet-to-wet. Wet-to-wet dressings need frequent dampening and are time-consuming to manage. They can be a reasonable initial choice for contaminated dry, scabby wounds.

Dressings are important for supporting autolytic debridement and maintaining an appropriate level of moisture at the surface of the wound.

Maggots

Medical maggots can be used to debride wounds. Fly larvae, or maggots, feed on living and/or necrotic tissue depending on the species of fly. Maggots of the greenbottle fly (*Lucilia sericata*) are used medically as they feed preferentially on dead tissue. The maggots are raised commercially in a sterile environment and can be applied directly to the wound, or contained in nets. Maggots produce enzymes that dissolve devitalized tissue and they feed on the resulting protein-rich liquid. They also kill bacteria and have been used to treat wounds infected with antibiotic-resistant bacteria, such as methicillin-resistant *Staphylococcus aureus* (MRSA). Maggots are generally used for a few days until the wound has the appearance of healthy, non-infected granulation tissue. They can then be removed from the wound and disposed of.

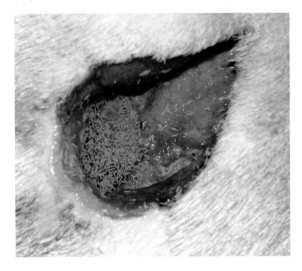

Medical maggots used in a wound for their debriding action. (Photo: A. Thiemann)

MANAGING AN OPEN WOUND

Clipping and cleaning the surrounding skin, then flushing and debriding the wound, are practical first steps, regardless of whether the wound will be sutured (stitched) together, or left to heal as an open wound. In an ideal situation a wound is sutured or stapled to bring the remaining tissue, with relatively normal architecture, close together. The body then has a very small gap to fill and repair, and lots of adjacent cells and nutrients available to make it happen. This type of wound healing gives a better functional and cosmetic result, requires a lot less management and occurs more quickly. Counter-intuitively, the cost of surgically closing a wound is often less than the accumulated cost of dressings and bandaging for an open wound.

Unfortunately, closing a wound is not always possible and we end up managing an open wound. This may occur when the surrounding tissues are too tight to move towards the wound, for example on the lower part of the legs, or when large amounts of tissue are missing, or when a previously repaired wound breaks down. Skin flaps and grafts may be helpful, to compensate for a shortage of immediately available skin to cover the wound.

Wound Dressings

Covering a wound has many benefits. The right amount of bandage pressure can reduce tissue swelling. A covered wound is protected from dirt, debris and bacteria in the environment, and from fly-worry and fly-strike. A cast or bandage can reduce movement within the wound, for example by restricting the mobility of a knee or fetlock joint, and can reduce self-trauma from biting or rubbing. The neoplastic change to sarcoid formation occurs more commonly in uncovered wounds, possibly related to fly attention. Covering a wound keeps it moist, which optimizes the healing process. The wound fluid provides a moist environment full of helpful enzymes. One of the aims in selecting dressings is to maintain just the right amount of wound fluid in contact with the wound. Granulation tissue forms more quickly when a wound is covered and moist. This is helpful until the granulation tissue fills the wound space. Ideally, it will then stop forming and epithelial cells will migrate across from the wound edges. Exuberant granulation tissue also forms more readily when a wound is dressed. A compromise, to reduce the risk of proud flesh formation (see later this chapter), can be to cover the wound until it is filled with granulation tissue, then to leave the wound uncovered, or to use a foam dressing, while the flat surface forms level with the surrounding skin, and the wound starts to contract. The next stage is to cover the wound again to provide a warm, moist environment for epithelial migration across the granulation tissue surface. Bandaging protects the delicate migrating epithelial cell layer, which is easily abraded by bedding material, or by hard surfaces in the stable. These three stages are, in reality, overlapping rather than linear so assessment and judgement is required for each individual wound.

Dressings with particular properties can be held in contact with a wound in any body location that will allow a bandage. There is a wide range of dressing options available, some of which are discussed below. Care should be taken with all dressings to match them to the changing nature and needs of the wound. The frequency of changing dressings will vary with the type of wound. Highly exudative wounds may need dressings changed every few hours, while wet-to-dry debriding dressings may be changed once a day. Dressings need to be held in place and are often bandaged. The pressure of a bandage is important to the success of wound healing. A dressing needs to be closely applied to the wound, without movement or underlying space. An overly tight bandage may compromise blood flow and cause swelling or tissue damage. The firm, even pressure, and warmth, of a good bandage can contribute to pain relief. Bandaging can stabilize the area and

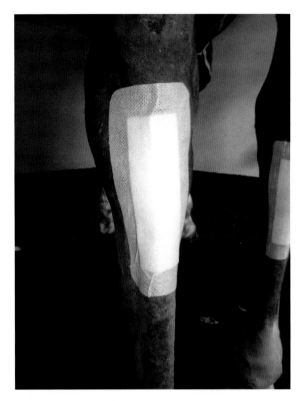

A sterile dressing placed over a surgical wound. The dressing has an adhesive border that sticks to the skin.

reduce the movement of tissues around the wound.

Some Types of Wound Dressing
Honey
Honey has an antibacterial effect. It has a low pH, and contains antioxidants which protect against free radicals. Free radicals are released during the healing process and can cause tissue damage. Honey tends to stick to the skin and forms a flexible layer. These qualities make it useful for wounds on sites that are difficult to bandage. Manuka honey is thought to have greater antibacterial potency than regular honey, although research has shown Scottish heather honey to have good antibacterial effects. The manuka tree (*Leptospermum*) grows

in New Zealand and Australia. Worldwide sales of manuka honey currently exceed the annual amount produced, suggesting that the contents of a pot may not match the label. Honey and sugar-based dressings draw water into the area and maintain a moist wound site.

Silver

Dressings containing silver are also antibacterial. They can be applied dry to an exudative wound, or wetted with sterile water before being placed onto a dry wound. Note that wetting a silver dressing with saline can inactivate it.

Hydrogels

Hydrogels have a soft, flexible, jelly-like nature. They conform to the body surface and can fill spaces in wounds. Hydrogels are made of a network of polymer chains which hold a large amount of water. They are useful for direct application to dry wounds. The hydrogel hydrates the wound and provides a moist wound environment, which is more conducive to healing than a dry one.

Foam

Foam dressings provide a soft insulation layer and increase the local wound temperature. They are generally used to encourage and protect the delicate epithelial layer after a healthy granulation tissue bed has formed. They can also be applied after proud flesh has been cut back, to inhibit the formation of further exuberant granulation tissue.

Hypertonic saline

Hypertonic saline dressings contain a high concentration of salt. Like honey and sugar-based dressings they draw fluid into themselves and have a debriding and antibacterial effect.

Calcium alginate

Calcium alginate dressings are derived from seaweed. They come as soft flexible pads. The pads are moistened with sterile saline before use on a dry wound surface, or applied dry to a wet wound surface. They are used on dry wounds to stimulate granulation tissue formation, and on weeping wounds to absorb large amounts of exudate. Alginate dressings do not stick to wound surfaces, mould easily over irregular surfaces and are easy to remove. They can also be pushed into bleeding wounds to help with blood clotting.

Poultices

A poultice is a soft, wet material applied warm or cold to the foot or skin. Poultice material is commercially available as a plastic-backed pad containing boric acid, a mild antiseptic, and tragacanth, a natural gum. The pad can be cut to size and used warm and wet on foot abscesses, or cool and wet on sprains and strains. Poultices were previously homemade using bran mash, soaked bread or porridge, to maintain warm or cool temperatures for extended periods. Poultices are not generally used on wounds.

Bandaging

Wound dressings are usually covered with a layer of cotton wool, or Gamgee (cotton wool covered with gauze). This middle layer can take up excess fluid that weeps from the wound. It is soft and conforms to the shape of the area. The middle layer provides insulation to keep the wound warm. It needs to be applied with enough pressure to stabilize the dressing over the wound, and without folds that would create uneven pressure.

The outer layer of a bandage is usually an elastic wrap which sticks only to itself. The cohesive bandage is applied with an even

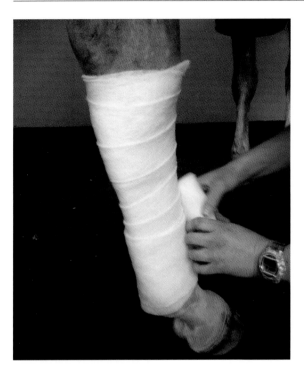

The first layer, of soft padded bandage, applied over a dressed hind limb wound.

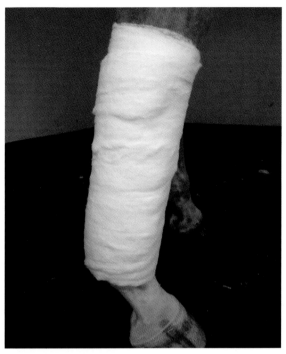

The second layer, of cotton wool, gives soft conforming bulk to the dressing.

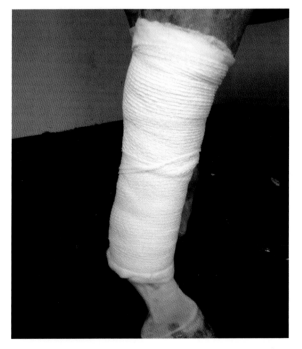

The third layer, of slightly elastic open weave bandage, compresses the underlying padding.

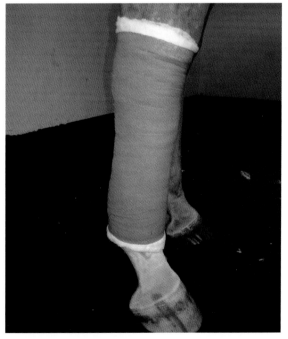

The fourth and final layer, of elastic bandage which sticks only to itself, compresses the underlying padding to give supportive but not excessive pressure.

pressure to hold the middle layer in place, and to compress the whole. A loose bandage may allow sagging and folding of the middle layer, and movement of the dressing; a tight bandage may over-compress the middle layer and contribute to pressure sores. Horses have a lot of sites where there is little tissue padding between the bone and the skin, especially on the head and legs. Great care is needed, when bandaging these areas, to avoid the creation of further skin wounds.

PROUD FLESH

The horse, in comparison to other mammals, is particularly prone to the production of exuberant granulation tissue. The tissue rises above the level of the adjacent skin, hence the name 'proud flesh'. Healthy granulation tissue has many useful roles. It fills the space of the wound and provides a framework within which further healing can occur. It contains lots of blood vessels, which carry oxygen, nutrients and white blood cells into the wound. Granulation tissue normally stops expanding when it is at the level of the surrounding intact skin. It provides a flat surface over which epithelial cells can migrate. Exuberant granulation tissue sticks up beyond the level of surrounding skin and makes it difficult for epithelial cells to migrate across. Proud flesh is not just an excessive amount of normal granulation tissue: analysis of its structure shows that the fibroblasts and blood vessels are haphazardly arranged, compared to the regular alignment in normal granulation tissue. Fibroblasts continue to divide and produce a random framework. The specialized type of fibroblast, which is capable of shortening in length, is less numerous and only has a haphazard orientation. Consequently the presence of proud flesh goes along with poor wound contraction. Good wound healing needs a brisk and efficient early inflammatory response, to bring in lots of white blood cells

---

FACTORS PREDISPOSING TO THE DEVELOPMENT OF PROUD FLESH

- Leg wounds are more likely to develop proud flesh when compared to wounds on the body, especially in areas of constant movement, such as over the joints. Frequent disruption of a wound, such as splitting of the granulation tissue when a fetlock flexes, prolongs the inflammatory phase.
- Horses are more likely to develop proud flesh than ponies, probably because of their less brisk and efficient early inflammatory phase. When ponies develop proud flesh it is likely to be less exaggerated, and to require less intervention.
- Areas with a poor blood supply are more at risk.
- Wounds that are infected, or have dead tissue in them, are more likely to develop proud flesh. Examples of dead tissue are sections of underlying bone or tendon which have lost their blood supply. Material from the environment, like a wood splinter or thorn, can also act as a focus for ongoing inflammation.
- Covering a wound, for example with a bandage or cast, increases the likelihood of proud flesh formation. This may explain some of the difference in the incidence of proud flesh between body and leg wounds. Body wounds are rarely covered, while leg wounds are routinely covered. On the positive side, bandages protect wounds from contamination and trauma. They keep the wound surface moist and provide a good environment for epithelial migration. They can also stabilize a wound that is too mobile.

and to clear away bacteria and unhealthy tissue. If this early inflammatory phase is inadequate, and leaves bacteria and contaminants in the wound, a low-grade chronic inflammatory reaction will rumble on.

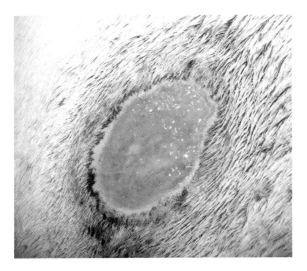

An elderly Highland pony with a large non-healing wound on the right flank. The granulation tissue has a pale, unhealthy appearance and it rises above the surrounding rim of pale-pink new skin. There is some pus on the surface of the wound, which is running onto the hair below. (Photo: M. Corke)

Treatment Options for Proud Flesh

- Check for complicating factors, for example underlying fragments of dead bone or embedded plant material.
- Cut away the protruding tissue. The proud flesh can be cut back to below the level of the surrounding skin. The surrounding skin margin, and any pink rim of new epithelium, is left undisturbed. This creates a new wound with a better chance of healing, although initially there is usually a lot of bleeding. Young granulation tissue does not have a nerve supply so this procedure can often be done with the horse standing and sedated. Very long-standing granulation tissue may have a nerve supply, so nerve blocks and/or

general anaesthesia may be needed before excision. It is worth keeping some of the removed tissue, in a pot of formalin, in case problems recur and there is a concern about the presence of a tumour. Sometimes the exuberant granulation tissue re-forms and has to be cut back again.
- Reduce surface contamination. The newly created wound surface is best covered to give a moist environment, and to prevent contamination with bedding material and dirt.
- Pinch-grafting of skin into the new granulation tissue can be helpful. It provides a greater surface area of 'edge' from which new epithelial cells can migrate, and can inhibit proud flesh formation.
- Reduce ongoing inflammation. Corticosteroid can be applied, once or twice, to the wound surface a few days after the proud flesh is cut away. The anti-inflammatory action of corticosteroids is helpful to arrest the chronic inflammatory process that produces proud flesh. It is not helpful to use corticosteroids more frequently, as they have the potential to inhibit the growth of new blood vessels, and to inhibit the migration of new epithelial cells.
- Ketanserin is a commercially available serotonin receptor antagonist. It comes as a gel and is helpful in lower leg wounds, a site where wound healing is often challenging. Ketanserin has been shown to reduce the formation of proud flesh and bacterial infection.

Treatments used previously, for example burning away proud flesh with copper sulphate, potassium permanganate or silver nitrate, are likely to be counterproductive. These caustic substances kill cells and leave dead tissue in the wound, which in turn stimulates an unhelpful chronic inflammatory response and delays healing.

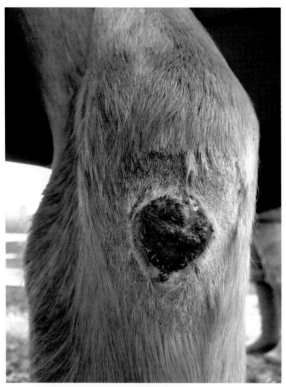

LEFT: *A wound at the back of the hock, caused by trauma while travelling in a horsebox. The wound has proud flesh and a warty appearance at the top edge. (Photo: V. Smith)*

BOTTOM LEFT: *The same hock wound two months later. The proud flesh is more pronounced and the horse occasionally traumatizes the area. Biopsy showed a mixture of proud flesh and sarcoid. The lesion was removed with laser surgery, followed by weekly application of imiquimod cream. (Photo: V. Smith)*

BELOW: *The same hock one year later. There is a healed, hairless scarred area. (Photo: V. Smith)*

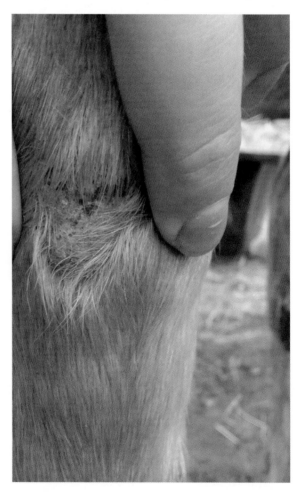

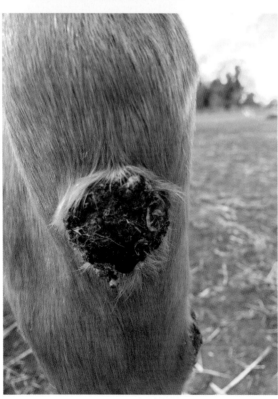

When is 'Proud Flesh' not Proud Flesh?

A rough-surfaced, irregular-shaped and expanding mass at a wound site is not always exuberant granulation tissue. Equine sarcoid, a type of tumour (see Chapter 6), can develop in a wound. Wound sites on the legs, especially towards the hooves, tend to develop the fibroblastic form of sarcoid. This form is easy to confuse with proud flesh. Wound sites on the body tend to develop the verrucose form of sarcoid, which has a rough, warty appearance. Horses that already have sarcoids, anywhere on the body, are more at risk of developing a sarcoid in a wound site. Less commonly, another type of tumour, squamous cell carcinoma, can occur at a wound site.

Wounds may heal with an excess of scar tissue. The amount of scar tissue may be disproportionately large compared to the size of the original wound. The roughened, matt and bumpy surface of excessive scar tissue (keloid) can be readily confused with the appearance of proud flesh or of a sarcoid.

SKIN GRAFTING

Most wounds, even large ones, will heal eventually. That healing may, however, take a long time and result in a lot of scarring. The horse may be out of action for an extended period. Scar tissue is generally less flexible and resilient than normal skin, and may restrict the movement of that part of the body. Cosmetic issues may also be important, as well as the costs of caring for a slowly healing wound. Skin grafting is a technique that moves living skin into the wound and, if things go well, promotes a faster, more functional and more cosmetic outcome. Skin grafting is particularly useful when we know that a wound cannot be closed by suturing or stapling, usually because too much tissue has been lost, or because the surrounding skin has low mobility. This is a common situation with wounds on the lower legs and the head. Skin grafting can help lower leg wounds to heal with good mobility around the joints, and head wounds to heal with a good cosmetic result.

The commonest type of graft used in horses is a **full-thickness** free skin graft from another part of the horse's own body. The term full-thickness means that, when the graft is cut out of the skin at the donor site, all of the depth of the dermis is taken. A **free skin** graft is free of any connection to the donor site. Its blood supply is cut when it is lifted out and it is a completely detached piece of tissue. Grafts can be taken from other horses, or even other species, but then the receiving horse will recognize the graft skin as 'not self' and mount an immune response against it. Such grafts are sometimes used as a sort of biological bandage for temporary benefit, even though they will eventually be rejected by the recipient's body. When we take a graft, we create a wound at the donor site, therefore it is helpful to choose a site that is not visually prominent, and which has mobile skin to allow easy wound closure. The side of the neck, under the natural lie of the mane, is a common choice. It is also at a convenient working height in the standing sedated horse. Taking the tissue in a regular and orderly way also produces a better cosmetic result at the donor site, for example taking punch grafts at regular intervals along the neck.

Skin grafts can be placed onto a fresh, clean wound, or a healthy granulation tissue bed. The wound site, in both cases, needs to have a good blood supply to support the graft, and to be free of infection and dead tissue. Even though a graft has a better chance of establishing on a fresh wound than on granulation tissue, grafting is often delayed until granulation tissue has formed. This is because a healthy wound will contract significantly, leaving a much smaller area to be grafted at the granulation stage.

Types of Graft

Punch Grafting

A biopsy punch is a device like a very sharp apple corer, a few millimetres in diameter. The technique of punch grafting uses a biopsy punch to remove plugs of skin from the donor site. A slightly smaller-sized biopsy punch is used to make holes in healthy granulation tissue, into which the plugs of skin are placed. The granulation tissue holes are made first so that the inevitable bleeding can stop before the holes are plugged. Since young, healthy granulation tissue does not have a nerve supply, the holes can be cut without local anaesthesia. By contrast, the side of the neck, from which the plugs are harvested, needs local anaesthesia. A larger biopsy punch is used to cut the plugs as they will shrink a little. It is helpful to lay the plugs out in an orderly way, on a damp sterile swab, as it is easy to lose track of the direction of hair growth once the small clipped and sterilized skin plugs are removed from the horse. Obviously it looks better to have the hair all eventually growing in the right direction at the recipient site. Approximately three-quarters of the punch grafts are likely to survive and a pale rim of new epithelial cells can be seen around each one after two to three weeks.

Pinch Grafting

Pinch grafts are made by pulling up a small wigwam of skin and cutting the base with a scalpel blade. The result is a circle of skin, about 3mm (0.1in) across, with a full-thickness centre and a thinner edge. Oblique slits are cut into the healthy granulation tissue that fills a suitable wound, and one pinch graft is slotted into each slit. This technique has a similar graft survival rate to punch grafting. Both pinch and punch grafts are best covered with a dressing that will not stick to the surface of the wound,

A 6mm biopsy punch, used for grafting.

and bandaged. The bandage presses the grafts down into the underlying tissue and stops fluid or air pockets from obstructing good contact of the graft with the wound. Both pinch and punch grafts are helpful for potentially mobile areas, for example over joints.

Sheet Grafting

A bigger piece, or sheet, of skin can be cut from the donor site, for example from the mobile skin of the lower chest area. This sheet of skin is sutured, stapled or glued onto a fresh wound, or onto healthy granulation tissue. The sheet can be made to cover a larger area by cutting slits at regular intervals to produce a slightly stretched lattice of skin. Sheet grafting gives a better cosmetic appearance than pinch or punch grafting as the result has more even hair distribution. The resulting skin is also more robust and resilient, as there is more continuous cover by normal skin. The bigger sheet of skin needs more oxygen and nutrients to survive, and has a lower graft survival rate than pinch or punch grafts.

Other grafting techniques are available, especially for large wounds, but require more specialist equipment and expertise.

12 Pills, Lotions and Potions – Treatments Used in Skin Conditions

Only limited numbers of drugs are licensed for use in the horse. Licensing a drug involves a large investment of time and money from a drug company. Not all skin conditions have an appropriate licensed drug available to use in their treatment. Veterinary surgeons in the UK are obliged to choose a licensed drug when one is available. They can go 'off licence' if the licensed drug is ineffective, or if nothing suitable is licensed. In these circumstances the cascade system of drug usage guides vets where to go next for a suitable drug. Vets can choose a drug licensed for the same condition in another animal species, or a drug licensed for a different condition in the same species. If there is still nothing suitable they can select a human medicine authorized in the UK, or import a veterinary medicine from the European Union. Finally they can prepare a medicine themselves, have one compounded by a pharmacist or import a drug from a country outside the European Union.

Drug companies sell drugs under brand names. These drugs have undergone research and development to show that they are effective and safe in the horse, at a certain dose, and for a named condition. Brand-name drugs have a known standard of safety and efficacy. They are sold at a premium price to allow the drug company to get back the significant amount of money that it invested in research and development. The drug company that invests in the initial work will take out a patent, usually valid for the first ten years of a drug's commercial life. When the patent period expires the drug comes 'off patent' and can be produced by other manufacturers. At this point the same drug often becomes available under a variety of different brand names and at lower costs. The drug may also be sold under its chemical drug name, with no branding, as a so-called generic product.

DRUG SAFETY

There is no such thing as a totally safe drug. The advice to 'first, do no harm' was thought to have been given to physicians by the ancient Greek Hippocrates. This sage advice highlights the potential for treatments to cause problems, as well as to solve them. There is a balance of risk, with every drug, between potential benefits and potential drawbacks. Each horse is an individual and, while the majority will tolerate a given drug, a small proportion will show adverse effects. These effects may be minor, and of little consequence compared to the benefits, but a small number of adverse effects may be serious. Drug data sheets, the leaflets in the box with the medication, often make dire reading. Data sheets are obliged to list all of the adverse effects that have been reported over time. It can be sobering to read the data sheet for a familiar human drug, such as paracetamol.

There is no one drug that is right for every horse. It is helpful to discuss your individual horse, his current problem and the medication options with your veterinary surgeon. Your vet can give a balanced view of risk versus benefit for the various drug options. The notes and comments on medication, both in this chapter and in the book as a whole, are intended to give a better general understanding of drugs and how they can be used. They are not a substitute for good professional advice from your local vet, which is tailored to the needs of your individual horse.

Using Medication Safely

A horse is a very large animal compared to a child or a dog, and equine dosages/quantities of medication could be very serious overdoses if consumed by a child or small animal. Try to store all medication in a safe place, preferably in a locked cupboard. It is helpful to keep drugs in their original packaging, with labels and data sheets attached. If drugs are accidentally eaten by a child or a dog, the relevant information is then quickly and clearly available to your doctor or vet.

It can be tempting to try out medication that has been dispensed for one horse on another horse. Many skin conditions have a very similar appearance but need very different medications! Always check with your vet before trying out an experimental treatment. Persistent skin issues benefit from a clear diagnosis.

TREATMENTS APPLIED TO THE SKIN

Bathing

Medicated shampoos need to be in contact with the skin for long enough to allow the active ingredient to be effective. Shampoos contain wetting agents, which allow the shampoo to contact the skin and hair. Wetting agents help to overcome the normally water-repellent nature of the skin and coat and allow the water/shampoo mixture to spread over the surface of the skin and hair. We know from experience that a horse takes a lot longer to dry after bathing with a shampoo than after being hosed down with water only. Water, without shampoo, has a high surface tension. This causes it to stick to itself rather than to the skin, and to form drops and rivulets that run away easily.

Leaving shampoo and water on the skin for too long can lead to over-hydration. We are familiar with skin over-hydration from when our finger pads become wrinkled after a long period in the bath. Medicated shampoos usually give clear guidance on the desirable contact time. It is helpful to use a timer to achieve an accurate contact time, since guessing a period of time is frequently unreliable.

FORMULATIONS FOR APPLICATION TO THE SKIN

A **gel** is a water-based, jelly-like, semi-solid material which spreads easily on haired and non-haired skin. Gels are readily washed off the skin by water and do not have a greasy texture.

A **cream** is a mixture of oil in water, with water making up the greater part. When the water part evaporates, a thin, greasy layer remains on the skin. Creams can have a smoothing and soothing effect on rough, dry and itchy skin.

A **spray** is a useful and time-efficient way of delivering liquids to relatively large areas of skin and hair coat. A spray bottle that generates sufficiently fine droplets, and an appropriate spray pressure, will penetrate the hair coat and cover the hair and skin with liquid. Spray formulations generally contain wetting agents to ensure good contact between the sprayed liquid and the skin and hair. Insect repellents are often applied with a spray, allowing widespread and even coverage of the skin.

A **shampoo** is a liquid containing a wetting agent and a cleansing detergent. It may also contain other active ingredients. Shampoo can be applied directly to the wet coat, or diluted in water before application. A contact time of several minutes is needed to allow the active ingredients to work, before the shampoo is washed away with water.

An **ointment** is a mixture of water in oil, with oil generally making up the greater part. When the water part evaporates a substantial greasy layer remains on the skin. Ointments can have a smoothing and soothing effect on rough, dry, and itchy skin.

A **powder** is a finely ground solid which can be puffed or shaken onto the skin in a fine layer. The skin and hair need to be dry before application, or the powder will form uneven clumps.

A **rinse** is made up with water from concentrate, then sprayed or sponged over the body. It is left on to dry, and not washed off. The active ingredient remains on the coat and continues to work over an extended period. Lime sulphur is used in this way.

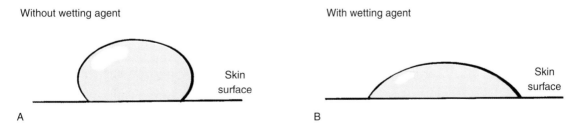

Without wetting agent   With wetting agent

Skin surface   Skin surface

A   B

A) A water droplet on the skin surface, without a wetting agent. The droplet is rounded and has little skin contact. B) A water droplet on the skin surface, with a wetting agent. The droplet is flattened and has a much increased area of skin contact.

Bathing the horse with a general shampoo can be helpful before the first medicated bath. This removes excess skin scale, dirt and grease, and allows the medicated shampoo better contact with the skin and hair coat. When the skin needs regular medication, and the horse has a long or thick hair coat, it is practical to clip out the coat before starting treatment.

Steroids (topical application)

Steroids are available in cream, gel and spray formulations for application to the skin. It may be helpful to clip the hair away from affected skin to allow easy treatment, but remember that hair can give the skin some protection if a horse is rubbing vigorously.

Different members of the steroid family have different levels of potency. The potency is affected by the type of steroid, for example betamethasone has a more potent action than hydrocortisone. Potency is also affected by the way the steroid is formulated, for example hydrocortisone aceponate is more potent than hydrocortisone. It is helpful to use the least potent steroid that will do the job, as it is likely to have the least adverse effects.

Repeated daily application of steroids can lead to thinning of the skin, and increased skin

---

SOME ACTIVE INGREDIENTS OF SHAMPOOS

Colloidal oatmeal is available in a variety of shampoos. It has a short-term action to reduce itching and can be very useful in managing flares of allergic skin disease. This drug has a good safety profile and can be used daily if needed.

Chlorhexidine. Shampoos are available with chlorhexidine alone, and in combination with other active ingredients such as miconazole. Chlorhexidine has antibacterial and antifungal (including anti-yeast) activity, depending on the concentration used. Solutions containing at least 2 per cent chlorhexidine are recommended as being effective against bacteria, *Malassezia* and ringworm. Chlorhexidine has some residual activity and will continue to work in the skin after the shampoo has been washed away. It can cause damage to the cornea, so it is important to ensure that shampoo does not run into the eyes. Some horses, and some people, will have skin irritation after contact with chlorhexidine. Wearing gloves is a sensible precaution when using this product.

Ethyl lactate has a mild degreasing action, and good antibacterial activity.

Selenium sulphide is available in a 1 per cent shampoo formulation. It has an excellent degreasing action, anti-parasitic and antifungal properties, and it acts on skin scale. Selenium sulphide loosens the attachments between surface skin cells (a keratolytic action), and causes scale to come away from the skin. It also slows down the turnover of surface skin cells (a keratoplastic action), so that scale is not so rapidly produced. Selenium sulphide shampoo is diluted in a bucket before use. It is important to prevent horses from licking or swallowing the solution. The solution is applied with a sponge and left on the skin for ten minutes before thoroughly rinsing off. Selenium sulphide can sometimes cause irritation and drying of the skin, and can discolour a pale hair coat. It is sensible to wear gloves when using the product, and it can discolour jewellery.

The words corticosteroid, glucocorticoid
and steroid tend to be used interchangeably,
but they actually mean different things.
The steroid hormone family contains both
anabolic steroids and corticosteroids.
Anabolic steroids have been used, for
example, by body-builders to enhance
muscular development. They are a banned
substance in most competitive sports.
The **corticosteroid** family contains both
glucocorticoids and mineralocorticoids. The
term 'cortico' tells us that these steroids are
produced by the cortex, or outer section,
of the adrenal gland. Glucocorticoids are
important drugs in dermatology. They are
mostly used for their anti-inflammatory
action. The term steroid is widely used to refer
to any of the glucocorticoids, and is used in
this context throughout this book.

In summary, the steroid family can be
viewed like this:

STEROIDS
— *Anabolic steroids*
— *Corticosteroids*
   — Glucocorticoids
   — Mineralocorticoids

fragility where the steroid has been applied.
This effect seems to happen most readily
on the skin of the lower legs. Most topical
preparations affect the skin and also, to some
degree, are absorbed into the horse's body. A
notable exception is hydrocortisone aceponate
spray which has good potency in the skin, but
is broken down to inactive derivatives before it
reaches the rest of the horse. Steroids should
not be used on broken skin as they are likely to
bring about a delay in wound healing.

Just as the drugs are active in the horse's skin,
they can affect people too. It is important to
wear gloves when applying them.

Antiseptics

Antiseptics kill a wide range of micro-organisms.
The two most familiar antiseptics in veterinary
medicine are chlorhexidine and povodine
iodine. Hypochlorous acid is perhaps a less
familiar antiseptic.

Chlorhexidine

As well as the shampoo formulation already
discussed, chlorhexidine is available in a skin
scrub formulation for use before surgery. Skin
scrub formulations contain detergents with
a degreasing action. They can be drying and
irritant to the skin if used frequently.

Chlorhexidine has antibacterial and antifungal
(including anti-yeast) activity, depending on the
concentration used. A 0.05 per cent solution,
of non-detergent formulation, can be used for
flushing wounds. Chlorhexidine should not
be used persistently on wounds as it can delay
healing, particularly during the epithelialization
phase. Take care not to get chlorhexidine into
the eyes as it can cause damage to the cornea.
Some horses may have skin irritation after
the application of chlorhexidine products, or
develop dry skin at the area of application.
Chlorhexidine has a residual action on the skin,
even after rinsing it away. Concentrations of
2 per cent, or more, are recommended for the
treatment of ringworm or *Malassezia* dermatitis.

Povodine Iodine

Povodine iodine is most often used as a
skin antiseptic before surgery. Along with
chlorhexidine and hypochlorous acid, povodine
iodine has good efficacy against bacteria, fungi
and yeasts at the appropriate concentrations.

It is less commonly used to treat skin disease as it can be more drying, irritant and can stain a pale-coloured coat. Povodine iodine has a residual action on the skin even after rinsing. A water-based solution of povodine iodine (not the detergent formulation) can be useful for treating skin infections around the eyes, as it is well tolerated by the cornea.

Hypochlorous Acid

Hypochlorous acid disrupts the cell membranes of bacteria, fungi and yeasts. Consequently, it has a broad spectrum of antimicrobial activity. A preparation of hypochlorous acid is available as a spray formulation and has a fast onset of action against microbes.

Other Substances Applied Topically to the Skin

Silver Sulphadiazine

Silver sulphadiazine is available as a 1 per cent cream. It kills yeasts and a wide variety of bacteria. This drug is especially useful for treating *Pseudomonas* infections. As only a limited number of treatments will be effective against *Pseudomonas*, it is part of our antibiotic stewardship to reserve the use of silver sulphadiazine for those cases that really need it, and not to use it as a general treatment. Silver sulphadiazine can slow down the granulation of wounds.

Aloe Vera

Aloe vera is a substance extracted from a number of plants in the Aloe family. It is widely claimed to have effects against bacteria, fungi, insect bites, itching and pain. Chemical analysis shows a number of potential active ingredients, but there are too few robust clinical trials to yet demonstrate reliable efficacy, or to recommend one product or concentration over another.

Dimethyl Sulphoxide

Dimethyl sulphoxide, commonly known as DMSO, has anti-inflammatory effects particularly when used for acute, rather than chronic, inflammation. It is an organic solvent and passes easily into and through the skin within a few minutes of application to the surface. Consequently, it can be combined with other anti-inflammatory drugs to deliver them more readily to deeper tissues than if they were used alone. Topical DMSO is usually well tolerated but some horses may react with red or dry skin, and may show discomfort after application. It is important to wear gloves when handling this product.

Sunscreen

Sunscreen products work to protect the skin from harmful ultraviolet radiation. They achieve this in two main ways. The active ingredients zinc oxide and titanium oxide form a physical barrier to protect the skin. They reflect light away from the skin surface. Other active ingredients form a chemical barrier to the skin. They absorb energy from the ultraviolet radiation and dissipate some of its damaging action. Some sunscreen products contain active ingredients with a combination of these two actions. Products with a high sun protection factor (SPF) will protect the horse for a longer time before ultraviolet damage occurs. Sunscreens need to be reapplied regularly and are particularly indicated on skin without protective pigmentation and/or hair cover. Products such as certain children's sunscreens, which are coloured and/or opaque, are useful as they show that they have been evenly applied to the skin.

Lime Sulphur

Lime sulphur has effects against bacteria, fungi and yeasts. It may also have effects against some parasites, reduce itching and reduce skin scale. It is mainly used as a twice-weekly rinse treatment for ringworm, and as a treatment for chorioptic mange mites (*Chorioptes*) or harvest mites (*Trombicula*). The solution is made up from concentrate in a bucket before use, then applied to the skin and hair coat with a sponge or spray. Be careful that horses do not lick or swallow the solution. Horses with a lot of skin scale or mud in the coat will benefit from a general cleansing bath before the lime sulphur rinse is applied for the first time. The lime sulphur solution is left on the coat to dry and is not rinsed off. Some of the drug's activity is caused by hydrogen sulphide, which has a characteristic 'rotten eggs' smell. This smell is usually much reduced once the hair coat has dried. Lime sulphur solution can stain jewellery and porous surfaces such as a concrete yard. It may also cause a temporary yellowish staining of pale-coloured hair and skin. Try to avoid getting solution into the eyes or onto any mucous membrane, such as the mouth or anus. Gloves and a protective apron are recommended when using this product as the odour can linger. If the skin becomes dry with repeated treatments, some liquid paraffin can be added to the solution. Note that liquid paraffin is a mineral oil, available from pharmacies and from your vet; it is *not* the same as flammable paraffin liquid used in lamps and stoves.

Imidazoles

Ergosterol is an essential building block of fungal cell walls. The imidazole drug family inhibits the production of ergosterol and consequently debilitates and kills fungi. The family has drug names ending in '-azole', for example clotrimazole and miconazole. Topical creams can be useful for treating localized ringworm and *Malassezia* dermatitis. An enilconazole rinse and a miconazole/chorhexidine shampoo are available for treating more widespread ringworm.

TREATMENTS GIVEN INTERNALLY TO THE HORSE, WHICH HAVE ACTION ON THE SKIN

The following are discussed in alphabetical order.

Allergen-Specific Immunotherapy (ASIT)

This method of treatment is also called desensitization, hypo-sensitization, allergy vaccine and, in the USA, allergy shots. ASIT starts with a loading phase, where slowly increasing doses of allergen are given over increasing periods of time. There is then the maintenance phase, when the same dose of allergen is given at a regular interval. If ASIT suits the horse, and is helpful in reducing the clinical signs, maintenance treatment can be continued for the rest of his life. Immunotherapy is allergen-specific, when the vaccine is made for the individual horse, based on the horse's history and location, the results of that horse's intradermal test, and/or on measurements of antibody levels in the blood. The specific allergens that are relevant for that horse are included in the vaccine. It is important that the vaccine fits the story of the horse. For example, a horse in the UK with seasonal itch in the late summer is unlikely to be assisted by a vaccine that contains only tree pollens, as tree pollens are prevalent early in the year.

ASIT works by exposing the horse, on a regular basis, to small amounts of the substance to which he is allergic. This results in the immune system becoming more tolerant, and less reactive, to the allergens in the vaccine. Tolerance takes time to develop and the efficacy of ASIT is usually looked at after eight to twelve months of the treatment. The amount of ASIT given, and the frequency with which it is given, can be tailored to the individual

SEASONAL TIMING OF ALLERGENS IN THE UK

Tree pollens. Alder and hazel (February), through willow, ash and oak, to lime (June).

Grass pollens. May to August, peaking in June and July.

Weed pollens. June to August.

Mould spores. Present all year round, but peak with damp conditions.

Storage mites/dust mites. Present all year round, but peak in warm, damp conditions.

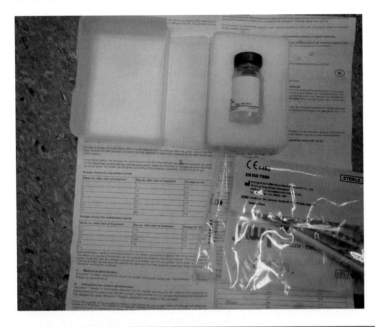

An allergen-specific immunotherapy kit. This vial of immunotherapy vaccine comes with an appropriate number of syringes with attached needles, advice about the safe use of the medication and a dosing schedule.

ADVANTAGES AND DISADVANTAGES OF ALLERGEN-SPECIFIC IMMUNOTHERAPY

Advantages
- The only treatment option that works on the basis of the disease.
- Effective for approximately seven out of ten atopic horses.
- Useful for competition horses where regulation restricts the use of certain drugs.
- Cost-effective.
- Good safety profile.

Disadvantages
- Rare cases of allergic reaction to the vaccine in the loading phase.
- Not effective for approximately three out of ten atopic horses.
- Needs organization, and time commitment, for regular injections by the handler.
- Vaccine vial needs refrigeration.

horse in consultation with a vet or a veterinary dermatologist.

ASIT is the only treatment option, of the many available for atopic dermatitis, that changes the basis of the disease rather than treating only the clinical signs. Successful treatment can prevent, or reduce, the development of clinical signs and can impact on the severity of disease over a horse's lifetime. ASIT can be used alone, or together with other treatment options, including steroids. Combined use can reduce the amount of drug therapy needed to make a horse comfortable. ASIT is a cost-effective long-term treatment option. The author recommends ASIT in almost all cases of atopic dermatitis.

Antibiotics

Antibiotics are widely used to kill bacteria. Unfortunately, bacteria can become resistant to the effects of antibiotics. Methicillin-resistant *Staphylococcus aureus* (MRSA) is an example. MRSA is resistant to the antibiotic methicillin, and to closely related antibiotics such as penicillin. MRSA can be carried by healthy horses and healthy people, in their noses. It can also be transferred between horses, and between horses and people, either by direct contact or by way of surfaces contaminated with the bacteria.

Resistance to antibiotics is a worldwide problem of great concern. The worry is that people and animals, including horses, will get bacterial infections that can no longer be treated with antibiotics. There is the potential to return to the problems of the pre-antibiotic era when some people and horses were very ill, or died, from common bacterial infections. Using antibiotics increases the likelihood of resistant strains emerging. The antibiotic-susceptible bacteria are killed, and the antibiotic-resistant ones survive and multiply.

It is important to strike the right balance between using these precious drugs when they are essential, and not using them when other treatments are an option. Many bacterial skin

GUIDELINES FOR USING ANTIBIOTICS IN HORSES

The British Equine Veterinary Association has drawn up a set of guidelines to promote the best use of antibiotic drugs. The guidelines are arranged within the mneumonic **PROTECT ME**.

Practice policy. Develop protocols for antibiotic usage based on common clinical scenarios. Classify key antibiotics as protected or avoided.

Reduce prophylaxis (giving antibiotics to reduce the likelihood of infection). Develop rational protocols for prophylaxis, for example surgical procedures. Rationalize disease control.

Other options. Reduce or replace antibiotics with other methods for bacterial reduction. For example, utilize wound debridement/lavage.

Types of drug and bacteria. Select appropriate drugs based on empirical use guidelines.

Employ narrow-spectrum antibiotics wherever possible.

Culture and sensitivity. Use bacterial culture promptly, especially when the clinical response to an antibiotic is less than expected or when long-term therapy is suspected.

Treat effectively. Give enough antibiotic for long enough, then stop.

Monitor antibiotic use, compliance and resistance.

Educate. Inform your team and your clients.

infections can be treated with antibacterial products applied to the skin, rather than by using antibiotics.

Antihistamines

Histamine is one of many chemical mediators involved in inflammation and itching. It is released in the body during an allergic reaction. Histamine needs to bind to a histamine receptor before it can contribute to inflammation and itching. Antihistamines also bind to histamine receptors: they compete with histamine for binding sites. Because of this, it is best to give antihistamines before an allergic challenge so that the binding sites are occupied before histamine is released.

Antihistamines have a low overall efficacy. It is not possible to predict which particular antihistamine will work for an individual horse, if at all. They belong to a number of families. It may be worth trying a member of a different antihistamine family if the first choice has no effect. Antihistamines can be helpful in some cases of recurrent urticaria and allergic skin disease. Chlorpheniramine, cetirizine and hydroxyzine have all been used in horses. Hydroxyzine, a first generation drug, is the most frequently used member of the group. First generation drugs have been around a relatively long time, have a lot of data available about them, and can cause sedation. Hydroxyzine is given, at first, three times daily by mouth. The dose can be tapered to twice or once daily as the condition comes under control. It should not be used in pregnant mares as it can harm the development of the unborn foal. Occasionally it can cause hyperactivity or changes in behaviour. Hydroxyzine may be more helpful in the treatment of recurrent urticaria than in controlling itching. It can be used in combination with other treatments, for example with allergen-specific immunotherapy and/or with steroids.

Pergolide

Pergolide works by binding to dopamine receptors. It mimics the action of dopamine in the body. PPID is thought to be triggered by falling dopamine levels in some older horses. Giving a horse pergolide replaces the effect of the falling dopamine levels and reduces the over-activity of the intermediate part (pars intermedia) of the pituitary gland.

Pergolide is the current preferred drug for treating PPID (equine Cushing's disease), and has a licensed formulation. It comes as a 1mg tablet, which can be divided to match the horse's bodyweight. The dose is given once daily by mouth, usually hidden inside a treat. The tablet should not be crushed, to reduce human exposure to the drug, but it can be dissolved in a small amount of water and poured onto feed.

Most horses will show some improvement after one month of treatment, and will continue to improve over subsequent months. The dose can be gradually increased each month, up to a maximum dose, if improvements are not seen. Some horses have a poor appetite, weight loss, behavioural changes and/or lethargy when the drug is first started, or associated with dosage increases. The appetite usually returns to normal after the first week of treatment, or after the first week of the new dose. If the appetite does not return to normal the dose should be reduced and, after a period, other causes of poor appetite can be considered.

When a good clinical response is seen, the dose can be reduced to the lowest effective level. This is the level that controls the clinical signs, and avoids adverse effects. Once horses are stable on treatment they can be monitored every six months by clinical assessment and blood testing. Pergolide has not been evaluated in breeding, lactating or pregnant horses and may interfere with reproductive hormones.

Steroids (Systemic Treatment)

The effects of steroids tend to depend on the specific one chosen, the amount given and the frequency with which that amount is given. A few horses will be sensitive to even very low doses. The names of drugs in the steroid family usually end with '-one', for example prednisolone, hydrocortisone, dexamethasone. These should not be confused with phenylbutazone ('bute'). Despite having the same '-one' ending, phenylbutazone is a non-steroidal anti-inflammatory drug.

Steroids are available as tablets, injections, spray, powder and gel. Oral steroids are generally given in the morning and with a feed. Low doses tend to have anti-inflammatory effects and are useful for inflammatory diseases such as atopic dermatitis. They are generally first given at the top end of the anti-inflammatory dose for some consecutive days, then tapered and given every other day. It is important to follow the 'every other day' dosing plan for long-term use. Such dosing allows the body to continue to produce its own corticosteroids, an ability that it is crucial to preserve for times of serious stress or illness. The long-term use of daily steroids suppresses the ability of the body to make its own steroids, and can lead to serious problems. Short-acting drug formulations given by mouth are preferable to long-acting injectable formulations for the same reason: that is, they allow the body to maintain its normal rhythmic production of steroids High daily doses tend to have immunosuppressive effects. These immunosuppressive doses are used to treat immune-mediated diseases such as PF. The idea is to treat at full dose until the disease goes into remission and then to slowly taper the dose. Horses receiving these higher doses will have some degree of suppression of their own ability to make steroids. It is, therefore, very important not to stop the drugs suddenly, as the body will be left without any steroids – either from within or without. Therefore, don't run out of pills, or miss a day's treatment, when on high doses. When the disease responds to treatment, the dose may be slowly tapered down. The slow taper allows the body to gradually resume its own production of steroids in response to the falling levels given by mouth. A slow taper also allows a maintenance dose to be identified. If the disease returns part way through the taper, we can try to maintain the horse on a dose of medication just above the one at which the disease came back.

THE RELATIVE POTENCY OF SOME STEROIDS

Glucocorticoid (anti-inflammatory) activity

Hydrocortisone	1
Prednisolone	4
Methylprednisolone	5
Dexamethasone	29
Betamethasone	30

Steroids affect most parts of the body, even when we only want to see a beneficial effect in the skin. The most common adverse effects are increased thirst and hunger, and passing more urine. Horses may put on weight if their food intake is not regulated.

A brisk and efficient inflammatory reaction is important for wound healing, and for dealing with infections. Steroids are potent anti-inflammatory drugs and can delay wound healing and increase the risk of infections. They can also have adverse effects on the liver. Systemic steroids are generally not recommended in horses with heart or kidney disease, or during pregnancy.

The use of steroids carries the risk of inducing laminitis, particularly in horses with pre-existing insulin resistance. Horses at risk of developing laminitis need careful attention to bodyweight, diet, footcare and exercise, especially if they are receiving steroids for other reasons. Long-acting injectable steroid formulations carry a higher risk of precipitating laminitis than short-acting forms given by mouth. The steroid action of long-acting forms cannot be stopped quickly if signs of laminitis occur.

NON-STEROIDAL ANTI-INFLAMMATORY DRUGS (NSAIDS)

These, for example phenylbutazone ('bute') and meloxicam, generally have little effect on itching.

References

What the Skin Does and How it Does it

Breidenbach, A., 'Peculiarities of vitamin D and of the calcium and phosphate homeostatic system in horses', *Veterinary Research*, vol. 29, 173–86

McDonald, R., *et al.*, 'Latherin: a surface protein of horse sweat and saliva', *Public Library of Science One*, vol. 4, e5726

Pritchard, J.C., *et al.*, 'Validity of indicators of dehydration in working horses: a longitudinal study of changes in skin tent duration, mucous membrane dryness and drinking behaviour', *Equine Veterinary Journal*, vol. 40, 558–64

Scott, D.W., 'Skin of the neck, mane and tail of the curly horse', *Equine Veterinary Education*, vol. 16, 201–6

Speed, J.G., 'The importance of the coat in Exmoor and other mountain and moorland ponies living out of doors', *British Veterinary Journal*, vol. 116, 91–9

Identifying Individual Horses by Sight

For information on the genetics of coat colour: www.vgl.ucdavis.edu/services/coatcolour

Parasites Affecting the Skin

Liebisch, A., *et al.*, 'Experimental studies on the longevity of mange mites of the species *Psoroptes ovis, Psoroptes cuniculi* and *Chorioptes bovis* off the host', *Deutsche Tierarztliche Wochenschrift* , vol. 92, 181–5

Rendle, D.I., *et al.*, 'Comparative study of doramectin and fipronil in the treatment of equine chorioptic mange', *Veterinary Record*, vol. 161, 335–8

Rüfenacht, S., *et al.*, 'Combined moxidectin and environmental therapy do not eliminate Chorioptes bovis infestation in heavily feathered horses', *Veterinary Dermatology*, vol. 22, 17–23

Smith, F.D., *et al.*, 'Estimating Lyme disease risk using pet dogs as sentinels', *Comparative Immunology, Microbiology and Infectious Diseases*, vol. 35, 163–7

Sweatman, K., 'Life history, non-specificity, and revision of the genus Chorioptes, a parasite of herbivores', *Canadian Journal of Zoology*, vol. 35, 641–89

Zenner, L., *et al.*, 'Evaluation of four manual tick-removal devices for dogs and cats', *Veterinary Record*, vol. 159, 526–9

Neoplasia Affecting the Skin

Knight, C.G., *et al.*, 'Equine penile squamous cell carcinomas are associated with the presence of equine papillomavirus Type 2 DNA sequences', *Veterinary Pathology*, vol. 48, 1190–4

Stadler, S., *et al.*, 'Successful treatment of equine sarcoids by topical acyclovir application', *Veterinary Record*, vol. 168, 187

Taylor, S. and Haldorson, G., 'A review of equine sarcoid', *Equine Veterinary Education*, vol. 25, 210 16

Skin Diseases Associated with Hypersensitivity

Bergvall, K., *et al.*, 'Pharmacodynamics of clemastine in healthy horses', *Veterinary Dermatology*, vol. 13, 211–29

Lorch, G., *et al.*, 'Results of intradermal tests in horses without atopy and horses with atopic dermatitis or recurrent urticaria', *American Journal of Veterinary Research*, vol. 62, 1051–9

Losson, B., *et al.*, 'Biting midges overwintering in Belgium', *Veterinary Record*, vol. 160, 451–2

Lysyk,T.J. and Danyk, T., 'Effect of temperature on life history parameters of adult Culicoides sonorensis (Diptera: Ceratopogonidae) in relation to geographic origin and vectorial capacity for bluetongue virus', *Journal of Medical Entomology*, vol. 44, 741–50

McDonald, L.G. and Tovey, E., 'The role of water temperature and laundry procedures in reducing house dust mite populations and allergen content of bedding', *Journal of Allergy and Clinical Immunology*, vol. 90, 599–608

Robin, M., *et al.*, 'Repellent effect of topical deltamethrin on blood feeding by Culicoides on horses', *Veterinary Record*, vol. 176, 574

Stepnik, C.T., *et al.*, 'Equine atopic skin disease and response to allergen-specific immunotherapy: a retrospective study at the University of California Davis (1991–2008)', *Veterinary Dermatology*, vol. 23, 29–35

University of Worcester pollen calendar: www.worcester.ac.uk

Wallace, J.C. and Vogelnest, L.J., 'Evaluation of the presence of house dust mites in horse rugs', *Veterinary Dermatology*, vol. 21, 602–7

Non-Contagious Skin Diseases

Rashmir-Raven, A.M. and Spier, S.J., 'Hereditary equine regional dermal asthenia (HERDA) in Quarter Horses: A review of clinical signs, genetics and research', *Equine Veterinary Education*, vol. 27, 604–11

Changes in the Skin and Coat that Point Towards Internal Disease

Donaldson, M.T., *et al.*, 'Treatment with pergolide or cyproheptadine of pituitary pars intermedia dysfunction (equine Cushing's disease)', *Journal of Veterinary Internal Medicine*, vol. 16, 742–6

Perkins G.A., *et al.*, 'Plasma adrenocorticotrophin (ACTH) concentrations and clinical response in horses treated for equine Cushing's disease with cyproheptadine or pergolide', *Equine Veterinary Journal*, vol. 34, 679–85

Wounds and Wound Healing

Carnwath, R., 'The antimicrobial activity of honey against common equine wound bacterial isolates', *Veterinary Journal*, vol. 199, 110–14

Wilmink, J.M., *et al.*, 'Differences in second intention wound healing between horses and ponies: macroscopical aspects', *Equine Veterinary Journal*, vol.31, 53–60

For information on MRSA in horses: www.thebellamossfoundation.com

Pills, Lotions and Potions

Törneke, K., *et al.*, 'Pharmacokinetics and pharmacodynamics of clemastine in healthy horses', *Journal of Veterinary Pharmacology and Therapeutics*, vol. 26, 151–7

Textbooks

Bowman, D.D., Georgis' *Parasitology for Veterinarians*, 10th edn (Elsevier, 2014)

Knottenbelt, D., *Pascoe's Principles and Practice of Equine Dermatology*, 2nd edn (Saunders Elsevier, 2009)

Lloyd, D.H., Littlewood, J.D., Craig, J.M. and Thomsett, L.R., *Practical Equine Dermatology* (Blackwell, 2003)

Scott, D.W. and Miller, W.H., *Equine Dermatology*, 2nd edn (Elsevier Saunders, 2011)

Shashak, T. and Theoret, C., *Equine Wound Management*, 2nd edn (Wiley-Blackwell, 2008)

Index